Excel 2003
Foundation to Expert Guide

Chris Voyse and Patrice Muse

Published by
Voyse Recognition Limited

March 2006

Voyse Recognition Limited • Century Business Centre • Manvers Way • Manvers
Rotherham • South Yorkshire • S63 5DA • 01709 300188
www.smart-pc-guides.com

HCR 5/06

005.36

First Published in Great Britain in 2006

Voyse Recognition Limited
Century Business Centre
Manvers Way
Manvers
Rotherham
South Yorkshire
S63 5DA
01709 300188

ISBN 1-905657-04-8

ISBN 978-1-905657-04-9

Section 1: Foundation Level Objectives

- Introduction to Excel
- Creating New Worksheets
- Inputting Information into a Cell
- Opening and Saving Workbooks
- Introduction to Custom Lists
- Working with Simple Formula
- Relative and Absolute Formula
- Formatting Options
- Print Preview and Printing Options
- Inserting Header and Footer
- Creating a Simple Chart

Section 2: Intermediate Level Objectives

- Naming a Worksheet and Navigation
- Analysing Information in different Worksheets
- Working with Multiple Sheets
- Generate 3 D Formula
- Freezing Panes and Split Windows
- Working with Different Charts
- Vertical and Horizontal Lookup Functions
- Inserting Comments
- Password Protection
- Filtering Data

Section 3: Expert Level Objectives

- Creating Range Names
- Creating Range Labels
- Auditing a Worksheet
- Using Watch Window
- Strings and Text Functions
- Logical Functions
- Outlining a Worksheet
- Data Consolidation
- Templates
- Scenario Manager
- Custom Views
- Pivot Tables
- Macros
- What is XML?

Table of Contents

Section 1: Foundation Level Objectives

- Introduction to Excel

- Creating New Worksheets

- Inputting Information into a Cell

- Opening and Saving Workbooks

- Introduction to Custom Lists

- Working with Simple Formula

- Relative and Absolute Formula

- Formatting Options

- Print Preview and Printing Options

- Inserting Header and Footer

- Creating a Simple Chart

Introducing the Excel Screen

Microsoft Excel 2003 is a spreadsheet application released by Microsoft that runs in a Windows environment allowing you to create and edit both small and large workbooks. It is user-friendly and easy to work with providing prompts to help you identify icons on the screen that you maybe unfamiliar with and takes you through the various functions within this application.

Tour of the Screen

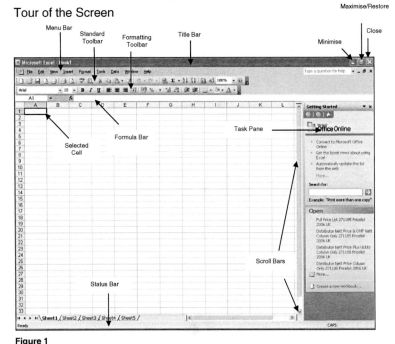

Figure 1

Title Bar

The Title Bar is highlighted in blue and defines the programme that you are in and the name of the Excel Workbook that you have opened. MS Excel will automatically display the default name, i.e. Book 1 in the Title Bar; once the workbook has been saved the saved name will be displayed in this area.

Menu Bar

The Menu Bar displays the drop down menus: File, Edit, View etc. This allows you to select the appropriate option that you require.

Standard Toolbar

The Standard Toolbar displays common features in Excel. The name of each icon is displayed when the mouse pointer is moved onto it.

Help

The Help icon can be found on the Standard Toolbar 🔘. Selecting the icon asks the question "What would you like to do?"

Formatting Toolbar

This displays icons that enable the worksheet to be formatted quickly.

Formula Toolbar

This toolbar is used for creating formula and displays the active cell.

Scroll Bars

Horizontal and Vertical scroll bars enable users to move around the workbook.

Status Bar

The Status Bar is at the bottom of the worksheet window. When the Caps lock key is selected, the word CAPS appears in the status bar area of the screen. This enables the numeric keypad area to be used. Click on the Caps lock icon to switch the feature off.

Drawing Toolbar

The Drawing Toolbar enables you to create two or three dimensional objects.

Sheet Tab

The Sheet tab \ Sheet1 / Sheet2 / Sheet3 / displays in white the active worksheet.

Task Pane

The Task Pane area appears on the right hand side of the screen and displays the various commands needed to perform such tasks as creating and opening documents, opening files stored in various locations, and a link to the general templates area. Other areas within the task pane are the Clipboard, Search Facility and Insert Clip Art. To view the task pane choose View, Task Pane. The task pane toolbar defaults to the New Workbook option, however this can be changed by selecting the downward arrow to the right of the text.

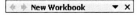

Figure 2

To switch between the task pane click on the downward arrow on the task pane title bar and select the required option. Use the arrow keys 🔘 🔘 🔘 to move backward or forward within the task pane area.

Opening Microsoft Excel

There are several ways that this application can be opened. On the desktop area of the screen, double click with the left ⌐⊕ button on the Microsoft Excel icon or select the Start Button **start**. Move your mouse pointer ⫩ over the text **All Programs** the Microsoft Excel ▦ Microsoft Office Excel 2003 icon appears. Click with your left ⌐⊕ button to open the programme.

Understanding Worksheets

Each new workbook contains three worksheets. If you required more worksheets you can alter the number of worksheets in a new workbook. To do this click on Tools, Options and on the General tab. In the screen print below, it displays Sheets in new workbook as 3, if you want to adjust the number of sheets select the required number and press [OK].

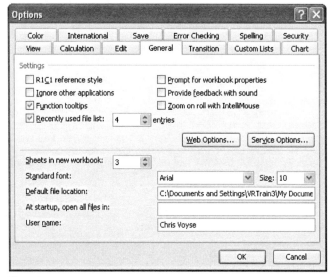

Figure 3

Moving around within a Worksheet

Excel references by a Column Reference and then a Row Reference.

1. Click in cell A1

2. Both the Column and Row reference are highlighted in orange

Figure 4

3. In the Formula Bar above Column A is the actual cell **A1**

4. When you select a cell a white cross appears

5. To select a cell click with the left 🖱 button

6. There are a number of fast ways to move to a different cell

7. Either use the arrow keys on the keyboard ⬇, ⬆, ⬅, ➡

8. This will highlight the next cell reference

9. Alternatively press the ⬛Tab⬛ key, the new active cell would be B1

10. To move back to cell A1, hold down ⬛Shift⬛, press ⬛Tab⬛

11. Click on cell A1 using the left 🖱 button

12. There are 256 columns in a worksheet from Column **A** to Column **IV**

13. To return to cell A1, hold the ⬛Ctrl⬛ and Home keys down

14. In cell A1, hold the ⬛Ctrl⬛ key down and select the ⬇ arrow

15. There are 65,536 rows in each worksheet

Inserting Information into a Cell

1. When you move the ⌇ pointer in a cell you see a cross ⌗

2. Move over cell G2

3. Click with the left ⌒ button to select cell G2

4. Type out the word January

5. As text is typed, the information appears in the Formula Bar and the cell

   | G2 | ▾ ✕ ✓ *fx* January |

   Figure 5

6. To accept the information in G2 either click on the green ☑

7. Alternatively, press the Enter key on the keyboard

8. Text entered into a cell automatically aligns to the left January

Editing Information in a Cell

Excel allows you to change information in several different ways. To go back a character, use the backspace key ⌫ on the keyboard.

1. Selected the cell to be edited

2. Press F2, a flashing curser appears to edit the cell contents as necessary

3. Alternatively, move the mouse over the cell you want to edit

4. As you move over the cell you will see a white cross

5. Guide the white cross over the cell to be edited

6. Double click with the left ⌒ button

7. The flashing curser appears where the cross was guided to appear

8. Edit the cell contents as necessary

Editing Information using the Formula Bar

1. Select the cell you want to amend

2. Move the left ⌒ button in the Formula Bar

3. Click with the left ⌒ button where the flashing curser is to appear

   | E3 | ▾ ✕ ✓ *fx* SMART PC Guides |

   Figure 6

4. Once amended click on the green ☑ or press the Enter key

Exercise 1: - Creating and Saving a Worksheet in Excel

Monthly Household Expenses	
Mortgage	£259.00
Rates	£27.00
Electricity	£13.00
Gas	£7.99
Television	£16.99
Telephone	£15.00
Insurance	£8.50
Food	£120.00
Total	£467.48

1. Open a New Workbook by selecting File from the Menu Bar and New

2. Select Blank Workbook

3. Type the text shown in Exercise 1 above

4. Click in the cell containing the title, press the bold B icon

5. Choose File, Save As from the Menu Bar

6. Save the Workbook with the filename EXPENSES.xls using the instructions on the following page

Saving a Workbook

1. Choose File from the Menu Bar
2. Select Save As

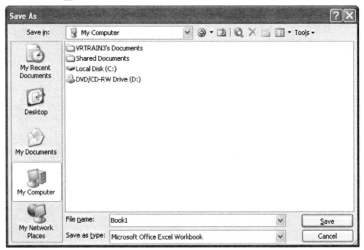

Figure 7

3. Type the filename in the File name box

4. Click on the My Documents folder My Documents

5. This takes the user to their personal workspace area

6. Alternatively select the required drive 3½ Floppy (A:) in the Save in box

7. Double click with the left button to open the required folder

8. The default is to save items as an Excel Workbook

9. Select Save

10. The Title Bar area displays the named Workbook

Saving a Workbook in a different format

1. Select File, Save As
2. In the File name area type the name of the file
3. In the Save as type box click on the downward pointing arrow

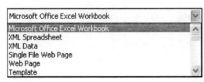

Figure 8

4. Select your chosen format, click [Save]

Opening a Workbook using the Menu and Keyboard

1. Select Eile from the Menu Bar

2. Below Properties on the pull down menu are the last 4 workbooks

3. Click with the left 🖱 button on the required workbook

4. This automatically opens the workbook

5. Alternatively using the keyboard

6. Hold the [Alt] key down, press the letter [F]

7. Use the downward arrow [↓] to highlight the required file

8. The bottom of the drop down menu displays the last four Workbooks

9. Select the required Workbook, press the [Enter] key to open automatically

Opening a Workbook using the Mouse

1. Click on Eile, Open from the Menu Bar or select the Open 🖼 icon

Figure 9

2. Choose the My Documents icon or the drive that contains the workbook

3. Double click with the left 🖱 button to open the required folder

4. Click the left 🖱 button on the individual workbook, press [Open ▾]

Opening Several Workbooks using the Control Key

1. Click on **F**ile from the Menu Bar or select the **O**pen 🗁 icon

2. Select the downward arrow [Look in: 🗀 Excel 2003 Foundation Course   ▾]

3. Choose the drive that contains the workbook

4. Double click on the required folder

5. Click the filename once with the left 🖱 button to select a workbook

6. Hold the [Ctrl] key down to select the next workbook

7. Each selected file is highlighted in blue

8. If a file is selected by mistake click again to deselect

9. Click [Open ▾] to open all the Excel workbooks

Opening Several Workbooks using the Shift Key

1. Click on **F**ile from the Menu Bar or select the **O**pen 🗁 icon

2. Select the downward arrow [Look in: 🗀 Excel 2003 Foundation Course   ▾]

3. Choose the drive that contains the workbook

4. Double click on the required folder

5. Click the left 🖱 button to select the first Workbook

6. Hold the [Shift] key down, click the left 🖱 button to select the last file

7. All selected files are highlighted in blue

8. Click [Open ▾] to display all the workbooks

Introducing Custom Lists

Why use a Custom List?

If you need to repeat information on a regular basis creating a Custom List is the best option.

Defining a Custom List

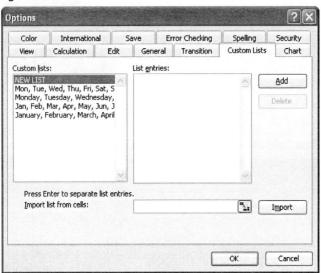

Figure 10

1. Select Tools, Options

2. Choose the Custom Lists tab

3. The left hand Custom lists dialog box displays the pre set lists

4. The right hand box is named as List entries

5. To define a new list click with the left ⌐⌐ button in the List entries area

6. Type out the list that you want to define

7. Press the Enter key after each list entry

8. When you have finished entering your list select the Add icon

9. The list is added to the Custom lists area

10. Select OK

Exercise 2: - Creating and Deleting a Custom List

The objective of this exercise is to define and reproduce information from a Custom List. Once created, the defined list can be reproduced in any worksheet.

| Customer Services |
| Human Resources |
| Logistics |
| Payroll |
| Purchasing |
| Research and Development |

1. Select Tools, Options

2. Choose Custom Lists

3. The left hand Custom lists dialog box displays the pre set lists

4. The right hand dialog box is named as List entries

5. To define a new list click with the left ⎙ button in the List entries area

6. Type out the details for each department on a different line

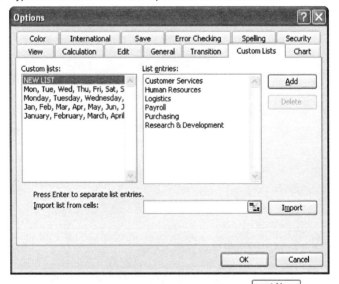

7. When you have finished entering your list select the [Add] icon

8. The list is added to the Custom lists area

9. Click on the [OK] icon

10. Click in a cell in any worksheet and type out Customer Services

11. Move the mouse pointer over the bottom right hand corner

12. The white cross ⌂ changes to a thin black cross

13. Click with the left ⌂ button and drag down six cells

14. The information to be placed in the next cell appears Human Resources

15. Drag over the required cells then release the mouse

16. To delete a custom list select **T**ools, **O**ptions

17. Select Custom Lists

18. In the Custom list area select the list to delete

19. The list is highlighted above

20. Select the Delete icon

21. The list is deleted from the Custom Lists area

Note: **It is not possible to delete the preset custom lists.**

Using the Undo and Redo Facility

When information is entered into a cell or a command is used, that information is stored in the memory. The Undo and Redo facility allows you to either go backwards or forwards on a step by step basis.

1. To undo an action click on the Undo [↺ ▼] icon

2. If you require to undo several steps, click on the downward arrow

3. Highlight over the steps that you want to undo

4. It is possible to go back a step if you have not saved the workbook

5. Repeat the same steps for the Redo [↻ ▼] icon

   Note: If you clicked on the downward arrow and selected the stage that you want to go back to it will delete all the steps.

Entering Simple Formula

1. Create the following data

	A	B
1		
2		
3	Regional Offices	Sales
4	Barnsley	26485
5	Derby	14000
6	Doncaster	23675
7	Leeds	34876
8	Leicester	8734
9	Manchester	12398
10	Nottingham	12876
11	Sheffield	3421
12		
13	Total	

Figure 11

2. To add up the sales figures in Column B

3. Select the cell where you want the answer to appear

4. All formula starts with equals [=] and the word sum

5. Type =Sum, press the opening bracket sign [(]

6. Once a bracket is open you can drag over the cells you want to add up

7. The cells are automatically referenced in the formula

8. If you open a bracket you must close a bracket [)]

SUM	▼	X √	ƒx	=sum(B4:B11	
	A	B	C	D	
1					
2					
3	Regional Offices	Sales			
4	Barnsley	26485			
5	Derby	14000			
6	Doncaster	23675			
7	Leeds	34876			
8	Leicester	8734			
9	Manchester	12398			
10	Nottingham	12876			
11	Sheffield	3421			
12					
13	Total	=sum(B4:B11			
14		SUM(**number1**, [number2], ...)			
15					

Figure 12

9. Creating your formula in this way means less typing and fewer mistakes

10. Alternatively type =SUM(B4:B11) or
    =SUM(B4+B5+B6+B7+B8+B9+B10+B11)

11. If you are using just one set of brackets and forget to close the bracket at the end of the formula, Excel will add this automatically

12. To complete the formula either click on the Green tick ☑

13. Or press the Enter key on the keyboard

14. The result displayed in cell B13 is 136465

15. Save the Workbook

Using the AutoSum Icon

SUM	▼	X √	ƒx	=SUM(B4:B12)	
	A	B	C	D	
1					
2					
3	Regional Offices	Sales			
4	Barnsley	26485			
5	Derby	14000			
6	Doncaster	23675			
7	Leeds	34876			
8	Leicester	8734			
9	Manchester	12398			
10	Nottingham	12876			
11	Sheffield	3421			
12					
13	Total	=SUM(B4:B12)			
14		SUM(**number1**, [number2], ...)			

Figure 13

1. Select cell B13, click on the AutoSum $\boxed{\Sigma}\boxed{\cdot}$ icon

2. The formula appears =Sum(B4:B12)

3. There is no information in cell B12

4. The AutoSum $\boxed{\Sigma}\boxed{\cdot}$ icon thinks you want to add up above B13

5. In this instance you do not want to select the cell B12

6. A dotted line appears around the area Excel thinks you want to add up

7. Move the mouse pointer into the middle of cell B4

8. Click and hold down the left button, drag to cell B11

9. A dotted line appears around the selected text

10. Click on the green tick $\boxed{\checkmark}$ in the Formula Bar

11. Alternatively press Return or $\boxed{\text{Enter}}$, on the keyboard

12. B13 contains the result 136465

Note: If you required a formula that needed a blank line to separate the total from the data, create the formula result first then insert a row above the total.

Using Multiplication Formula

	A	B	C	D
1		Monthly Salary	Tax	Net Income
2	Simon Cave	£3,500.00		
3	Paul Spandler	£1,210.00		
4	Joan Wood	£780.00		
5	Alison Muratore	£930.00		

Figure 14

The following steps display an easy way to create the multiplication formula. To multiply, Excel uses the multiplication icon, i.e. the asterisks $\boxed{*}$ button. Remember all formula starts with $\boxed{=}$

1. Select cell C2, press $\boxed{=}$

2. Click in cell B2 (notice the formula bar displays the reference)

3. Alternatively type out B2

4. Use the multiplication sign $\boxed{*}$ and type the TAX rate (in this case 20%)

5. The correct formula is $\boxed{\text{SUM} \quad \blacktriangledown \; \times \; \checkmark \; f_x \;\; \text{=B2*20\%}}$

6. Click on the green tick $\boxed{\checkmark}$ in the formula bar to stay in the cell

7. The information displayed in cell C2 should be £700.00

8. In cell C2, click on the black cross Fill Handle in bottom right hand corner, drag over cells C3, C4 and C5

9. This formula is a relative reference (this means the formula is relative to each column and each row)

C5	▼	*fx* =B5*20%		
	A	B	C	D
1		Monthly Salary	Tax	Net Income
2	Simon Cave	£3,500.00	£700.00	
3	Paul Spandler	£1,210.00	£242.00	
4	Joan Wood	£780.00	£156.00	
5	Alison Muratore	£930.00	£186.00	

Figure 15

10. This results appear in cells C3 to C5

Using Subtraction

	A	B	C	D
1		Monthly Salary	Tax	Net Income
2	Simon Cave	£3,500.00	£700.00	
3	Paul Spandler	£1,210.00	£242.00	
4	Joan Wood	£780.00	£156.00	
5	Alison Muratore	£930.00	£186.00	

Figure 16

1. Click in cell D2, all formula starts with ⊟, either type B2-C2 or

2. Press the ⊟ key, click in cell B2, press the ⊡ sign and click in C2

3. The cell reference is placed in the formula bar, press the Enter key on the

D2	▼	*fx* =B2-C2		
	A	B	C	D
1		Monthly Salary	Tax	Net Income
2	Simon Cave	£3,500.00	£700.00	£2,800.00
3	Paul Spandler	£1,210.00	£242.00	
4	Joan Wood	£780.00	£156.00	
5	Alison Muratore	£930.00	£186.00	

Figure 17

4. Move the mouse pointer over the bottom right hand corner of D2

5. Click with the left ⌧ button on the black Fill Handle, drag down to cell D5

6. The results appear in cells D3 to D5

Using Division

Excel uses the forward slash key 🔲 to divide information

D2	▼	*fx*		
	A	B	C	D
1		Amount Borrowed	Repayment Period of Loan	Monthly Cost
2	Car Loan	£4,500.00	48	
3	Car Loan	£21,500.00	36	
4	Car Loan	£13,750.00	24	
5	Car Loan	£11,250.00	24	

Figure 18

1. Select cell D2, press ⌐=⌐

2. Click in cell B2 or type B2 in the formula, press ⌐/⌐

3. Click in cell C2 or type C2 ⌐ SUM ▼ X ✓ ƒx =B2/C2⌐

4. Press the ⌐Enter⌐ key

5. The result in cell D2 should be £93.75

6. Use the black Fill Handle to drag the results for D3, D4 and D5

Using the Functions Sum, Min, Max, Average

Excel lets you quickly calculate the minimum, maximum, and average result of statistical information. The function name used to add information together is **sum**.

	A	B	C	D	E
1		£25,678	£5,679	£25,762	£5,643
2		£87,905	£765	£86,257	£79,233
3		£567,900	£46,870	£67,543	£29,858
4		£76,549	£6,874	£26,718	£54,289
5		£79,567	£89,643	£79,567	£67,528
6					
7	Total	£837,599	£149,831	£285,847	£236,551
8	Min				
9	Max				
10	Average				
11	Count				

Figure 19

1. Select a new workbook and type out the information in Rows 1 - 5 above

2. Type the words in cells A7 to A11

3. Click with the left 🖱 button in cell B7

4. Create the formula in cell B7, copy it across to cells C7, D7 and E7

5. Select cell B8

6. All formula starts with ⌐=⌐

7. Instead of using the word Sum use the word Min

8. Insert the bracket sign **(**

9. Click with the left 🖱 button in cell B1

10. A dotted line appears around the cell

11. Hold the left 🖱 button down and drag down to cell B5

SUM	▾	✕ ✓	*fx*	=min(B1:B5)	
	A	B	C	D	E
1		£25,678	£5,679	£25,762	£5,643
2		£87,905	£765	£86,257	£79,233
3		£567,900	£46,870	£67,543	£29,858
4		£76,549	£6,874	£26,718	£54,289
5		£79,567	£89,643	£79,567	£67,528
6					
7	Total	£837,599	£149,831	£285,847	£236,551
8	Min	=min(B1:B5)			
9	Max				
10	Average				
11	Count				

Figure 20

12. The formula states =min(B1:B5 in the cell and the formula bar

13. Close the bracket sign **)**

14. Click on the green tick ☑ to stay in cell B8

15. Move the mouse pointer ⟋ to the bottom right hand corner of cell B8

16. Use the black Fill Handle, click the left button and drag over C8 to E8

17. Release the left button

18. The formula is copied to the cells

19. Now create the formula for the Rows 9 to 11

	A	B	C	D	E
1		£25,678	£5,679	£25,762	£5,643
2		£87,905	£765	£86,257	£79,233
3		£567,900	£46,870	£67,543	£29,858
4		£76,549	£6,874	£26,718	£54,289
5		£79,567	£89,643	£79,567	£67,528
6					
7	Total	£837,599	£149,831	£285,847	£236,551
8	Min	£25,678	£765	£25,762	£5,643
9	Max	£567,900	£89,643	£86,257	£79,233
10	Average	£167,520	£29,966	£57,169	£47,310
11	Count	5	5	5	5

Figure 21

20. Save the Workbook Working with Total Min Max and Average Formula.xls

Using the Insert Functions Feature

If you were working in a workbook and forgot the function name of a formula, Excel provides a quick and easy access.

	A	B	C	D	E
1		£25,678	£5,679	£25,762	£5,643
2		£87,905	£765	£86,257	£79,233
3		£567,900	£46,870	£67,543	£29,858
4		£76,549	£6,874	£26,718	£54,289
5		£79,567	£89,643	£79,567	£67,528
6					
7	Total	£837,599	£149,831	£285,847	£236,551
8	Min	£25,678	£765	£25,762	£5,643
9	Max				
10	Average				
11	Count				

Figure 22

1. Click the left ⌐🖰 button in the cell where the results are to appear B9

2. Select the word **I**nsert, choose *fx* <u>F</u>unction...

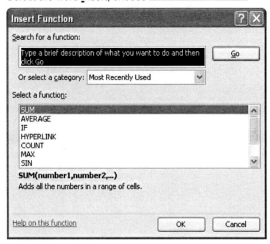

Figure 23

3. Select **S**earch for a function

4. Type the required function in this case max

5. Choose <u>Go</u>

Figure 24

6. Note the description is displayed below the selection

7. Click [OK]

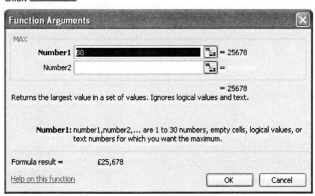

Figure 25

8. Select the dialog box 🔣 icon, click in the centre of cell B1 and drag to B5

9. Displayed in the Formula Bar is =max(B1:B5)

Figure 26

10. Select the dialog box 🔲 icon, click [OK] to display the results

Note: Alternatively to insert a function select the function 🔣 icon on the formula bar.

Exercise 3: - Consolidation Working with Formulas

	A	B	C	D	E
1	**Name**	**Salary**	**Monthly**	**Tax**	**Total**
2	Wright	£16,570.00	£1,380.83	£241.65	£1,139.19
3	Broad	£57,000.00	£4,750.00	£831.25	
4	Parratt	£85,600.00	£7,133.33	£1,248.33	
5	Martin	£16,000.00	£1,333.33	£233.33	
6	Christian	£14,750.00	£1,229.17	£215.10	
7	Nichols	£17,800.00	£1,483.33	£259.58	
8	Layne	£16,870.00	£1,405.83	£246.02	
9	Kirby	£13,200.00	£1,100.00	£192.50	
10	Roberts	£22,000.00	£1,833.33	£320.83	
11	Davidson	£11,250.00	£937.50	£164.06	
12					
13	**Totals**				
14	**Maximum**				
15	**Minimum**				
16	**Average**				
17	**Count**				

1. Open a new workbook

2. Create the information shown in columns A and B

3. In cell C1 type Monthly, in D1 type Tax and in E1 type Total

4. Click in cell B13 and create a formula to calculate the salary total

5. Create individual formulas for cell B14 – B17

6. Select C2 and create a formula to calculate the monthly salary

7. Use the Fill Handle to copy the relative formula to C11

8. Type Tax in cell F1

9. In cell F2 type 17.5%

10. Create a formula to display the monthly tax paid by each person

11. In Column E work out the monthly take home pay for each person

12. Save the exercise as Working with different formulas

Moving Information in a Worksheet

Information can be moved in different ways in Excel by using the Menu Bar options, the mouse, or the keyboard shortcuts.

Using Menu Bar Options to Move Information

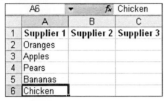

Figure 27

To move the information in cell A6 to B2

1. Select cell A6

2. Choose **E**dit Cu**t** [✂ Cut   Ctrl+X]

3. A moving dotted line appears around the selected cell

4. Click in cell B2

5. Select **E**dit, **P**aste [📋 Paste   Ctrl+V]

6. The information from cell A2 is moved to cell B2

Note: Cut and Paste icons on the Menu Bar display the shortcut keys Ctrl X and Ctrl V.

Using the Standard Toolbar Icons to Move Information

Moving information in cells A6 to B1

1. Choose cell A6

2. Select the Cut [✂] icon

3. A moving dotted line appears around the selected cell

4. Click in cell B2

5. Select the Paste [📋▾] icon

6. The information from cell A2 is moved to cell B2

Note: To use the right mouse button follow the same steps selecting the required icon.

Using Keyboard Shortcuts to Move Information

1. Select cell A6
2. Hold down the Ctrl key and select X
3. A moving dotted line appears around the selected cell
4. Click in cell B2
5. Hold down the Ctrl key and select V
6. The information from cell A2 is moved to cell B2

Using the Drag and Drop feature to Move Information

A6	▼	f_x	Chicken

	A	B	C
1	Supplier 1	Supplier 2	Supplier 3
2	Oranges		
3	Apples		
4	Pears		
5	Bananas		
6	Chicken		

Figure 28

1. Select cell A6
2. Move the mouse pointer ℞ over the left hand corner of the cell A6
3. A white pointing arrow appears
4. Click and hold down the left 🖱 button and drag
5. The left hand corner of the status bar states Drag to move cell contents
6. Keeping the left 🖱 button down, drag to the new destination
7. Release the left 🖱 button in cell B2
8. The information from cell A2 is moved to cell B2

Copying Information in a Worksheet

Using Menu Bar Options to Copy Information

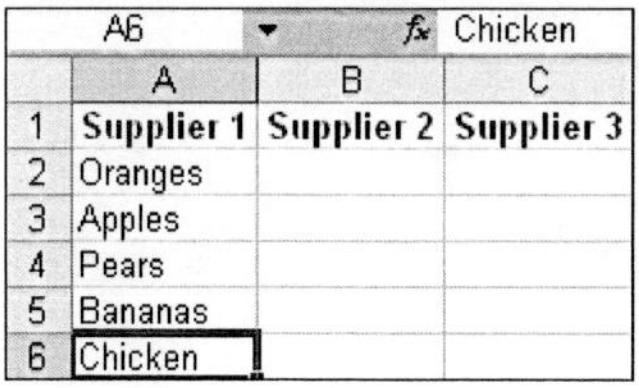

Figure 29

Coping information in cell A6 to B2

1. Highlight the cell reference you want to copy
2. Select **E**dit **C**opy [Copy   Ctrl+C]
3. A moving dotted line appears around the selected cell
4. Click with your left ☝ button to select the new cell
5. Select **E**dit, **P**aste [Paste   Ctrl+V]
6. The information from cell A6 is copied to the new cell B2
7. The moving dotted line still appears
8. To switch off the dotted line, press [Enter] or the Esc key on the keyboard
9. The information has been copied from cell A6 to B2

Note: Cut and Paste icons on the Menu Bar display the shortcut keys Ctrl X and Ctrl V.

Using the Standard Toolbar Icons to Copy Information

Coping information in cells A6 to B2

1. Highlight cell A6
2. Select the Copy ▣ icon
3. A moving dotted line appears around the selected cell
4. Click with your left ☝ button to select the new cell B2
5. Select the Paste ▣▾ icon
6. The information from cell A6 is copied to cell B2
7. To switch off the dotted line, press [Enter] or the Esc key

Note: To use the right mouse button follow the same steps selecting the required icon.

Using Keyboard Shortcuts to Copy Information

1. Highlight cell A6
2. Hold down the ⌈Ctrl⌉ key and select ⌈C⌉
3. A moving dotted line appears around the selected cell
4. Click with your left ⌐◻ button to select the new cell B2
5. Hold down the ⌈Ctrl⌉ key and select ⌈V⌉
6. The information from cell A6 is copied to cell B2
7. To switch off the dotted line, press ⌈Enter⌉ or the Esc key

Using the Drag and Drop Feature to Copy Information

A6	▾	fx Chicken
	A	B	C
1	Supplier 1	Supplier 2	Supplier 3
2	Oranges		
3	Apples		
4	Pears		
5	Bananas		
6	Chicken		

Figure 30

1. Highlight cell A6
2. Move the mouse pointer ⩗ over the left hand corner of the cell A6
3. Hold down the ⌈Ctrl⌉ key and the left ⌐◻ button
4. A plus sign + appears above the white arrow when the ⌈Ctrl⌉ key is down
5. The bottom left hand corner of the Status Bar states ⌈Drag to copy cell contents⌉
6. Drag with the ⩗ pointer to the new location
7. Release the left ⌐◻ button before the ⌈Ctrl⌉ key
8. The information in cell A6 has been copied to the new cell
9. Hold down the ⌈Ctrl⌉ key and the left ⌐◻ button

BODMAS

What is BODMAS?

BODMAS is the mathematical method that Excel uses to calculate a formula.

Name	Description	Symbol
B	Brackets	( )
O	To The Power of	^
D	Division	/
M	Multiplication	^
A	Addition	+
S	Subtraction	-

Figure 31

Excel always uses the BODMAS rule to work out information in brackets before it completes the multiplication part of the formula.

To work out the answer to "what is 5+2*10?"

Using the BODMAS rule, Excel will work out the multiplication part of the formula before the 5+2, however if the formula is = (5+2)*10 then Excel will work out the information in brackets first and then multiply the result by 10.

Different Types of References

Reference	Description of Reference
$A$1	Defines always look at Column A and Row 1
A$1	Defines always look at Row 1 but not Column A
$A1	Defines always look at Column A but not Row 1
A1	This is a normal cell reference

Figure 32

Excel uses four different types of references when working with formula.   To change the reference you need to type in a formula.

1. Click in the Formula Bar on the cell reference that you want to change

2. Press F4 slowly four times

3. The reference goes through the four different cell reference options

4. Alternatively type out the reference

Absolute Cell Referencing

Absolute Cell Referencing saves time when working in Excel. For example, if the VAT rate or a commission rate has been changed, Absolute Cell Referencing is a quick method of changing the reference that the formula is working to. The formula automatically updates information referenced in the cell.

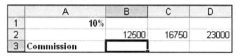

	A	B	C	D
1	10%			
2		12500	16750	23000
3	Commission			

Figure 33

1. By creating the formula =B2*A1 Excel works out 10% of 12500

2. In a relative formula you could drag across using the Fill Handle

3. If applied the results would be cell C3 zero and cell D3 zero

4. That is because no absolute cell reference has been applied

5. (In this example) absolute means "when applying the formula always look at cell A1"

6. To make a cell reference absolute use the following steps

7. Select cell B3

8. Click in the Formula Bar after =B2*A1, the flashing cursor appears

9. Press F4, dollar signs appear around A1

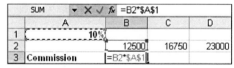

SUM ▼ X ✓ ƒx =B2*$A$1

	A	B	C	D
1	10%			
2		12500	16750	23000
3	Commission	=B2*$A$1		

Figure 34

10. Think of the dollar sign as saying "always look at Column A and always look at Row 1"

11. Select the Green tick ☑ to update the formula and stay in the cell

12. Use the Fill Handle to drag across C3 and D3

13. The formula in cell C3 is =C2*$A$1

14. The formula in cell D3 is =D2*$A$1

Formatting Options

The Formatting Toolbar is a quick way to apply different formatting options to your worksheet.

Formatting Toolbar

Figure 35

1. Select the cells that you want to format

2. Click on the downward arrow on the Font [Arial] icon

3. Change the name of the font to Times New Roman

4. Click on the Font Size [10] icon

5. Change the Font Size to 14

Description of the Formatting Toolbar Icons

Icon	Descriptive Prompt
B	**Makes selected text and numbers bold**
I	*Makes selected text and numbers italic*
<u>U</u>	Makes selected text and numbers underlined
≣	Aligns the selected text, numbers, or inline objects to the left
≣	Centres the selected text, numbers, or inline objects
≣	Aligns the selected text, numbers, or inline objects to the right
⊞	Merge and Centre
	Currency Icon
%	Percentage Style
,	Comma Style
.0 .00	Increase and Decrease Decimal point
≇ ≇	Decrease and Increase Indents
⊞	Borders
♢	Fill Colour
A	Font Colour

Figure 36

Using the Formatting Icons

The Borders icon adds or removes a border around selected text.

1. Click on the Border icon to display the different types of borders

Figure 37

2. Choose **D**raw Borders icon to select the thickness and colour of the border

Figure 38

3. Select the Line Colour icon to define a border, or

4. Choose **D**raw Border to define the border

5. Select **D**raw Border Grid to define the grid lines

Figure 39

6. Select the Erase icon to delete a border

7. Click on the Fill Colour icon to define the background colour of a cell

8. Choose the Font Colour icon to change the colour of the information in a cell

Formatting using the Menu Options

You can format your worksheet using the F**o**rmat C**e**lls option using the Menu Bar. Excel automatically chooses the general format when you open a workbook. You must select the cell(s) before you format information.

1. To change the formats highlight the cells to be formatted

2. Select F**o**rmat

3. Choose C**e**lls

4. Click on the Number tab

Figure 40

5. Select the required **C**ategory

6. Click on [OK]

Aligning Information

1. Select the required cell(s)
2. Choose F**o**rmat
3. Click on C**e**lls
4. Click on the Alignment tab

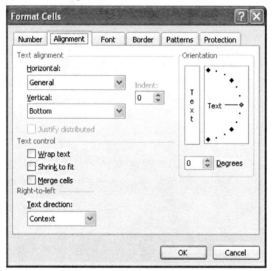

Figure 41

5. Change the **H**orizontal and **V**ertical options to center
6. Alter the orientation of text by clicking on the degree arrows
7. To change text control choose **W**rap text, Shrin**k** to fit or **M**erge cells
8. Orientation enables text information to be displayed at an angle
9. Input the number of degrees
10. Click on OK

Excel 2003 Foundation to Expert Guide

Format Text using the Font Tab

1. Select the required cell(s)
2. Choose Format
3. Click on Cells

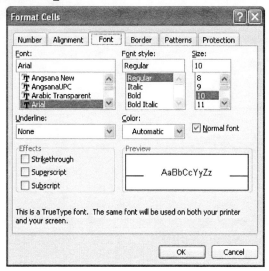

Figure 42

4. Choose Font to alter the font
5. Repeat these steps to change the Font style, Size, Underline and Colour
6. Strikethrough, Superscript and Subscript are special alignment options
7. The preview area display the selected options
8. Click on [OK] to apply the changes to the selected area

Add or Remove Borders

1. Highlight the area where you want a border
2. Select Format
3. Click on Cells
4. Select the Border tab

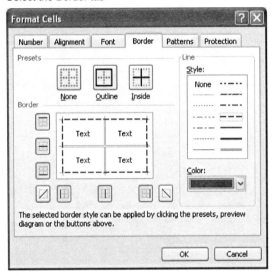

Figure 43

5. Click on the Presets, Preview Diagram or the buttons to select the border
6. Select Style
7. For a coloured border click on Colour
8. Click on the Preset icons or Border icons to add or remove the borders
9. A preview is displayed
10. Click on [OK] to apply the borders to the selected area

Note: If you want a different coloured internal border or style, select the line style and the colour, click on the internal borders icon, the preview area shows both colours and border styles.

The Patterns Tab

This tab sets the background colour of the highlighted area.

1. To format text using the Patterns tab

2. Select F**o**rmat

3. Click on C**e**lls

4. Select the Patterns tab

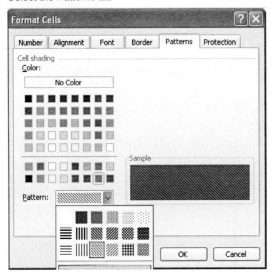

Figure 44

5. Click on Cell shading, **C**olour

6. Choose the colour required

7. Follow these steps to select a **P**attern

8. View your choice in the Sample area

9. Click on [OK] to apply the changes to the selected area

Format Painter Icon

Use the Format Painter [icon] icon to copy the format of a cell.

1. Select the cell you want to copy
2. Move the mouse pointer [pointer] to the Format Painter [icon] icon
3. Double click on the [icon] icon to apply the format to multiple cells
4. When switched on the Format Painter icon is indented [icon]
5. When moving over the cell you will see a white cross and brush
6. A dotted line appears around the original cell
7. Click with the left [button] button in the cell you want to apply the format
8. The format is changed to that of the original cell
9. Switch the Format Painter off by selecting the icon again so
10. The dotted line disappears when the facility is switched off
11. Selecting the [icon] once enables a user to apply a format once
12. When the cell or area is selected the Format Painter automatically switches itself off

Page Setup Options

Page Setup Options allow changes to the Page, Margins, Header/Footer and the Worksheet.

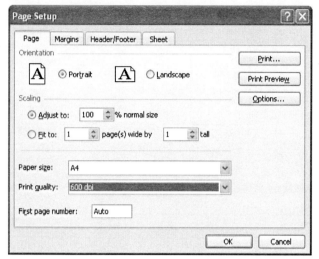

Figure 45

1. Select File, Page Setup
2. Choose the Page tab
3. Click on Portrait or Landscape to change the orientation of a worksheet
4. Click on the Paper size arrow to select the required size
5. Select [Print Preview] to view your worksheet
6. Click on the [Setup...] icon to return to the Page Set up dialog box

Margins Tab

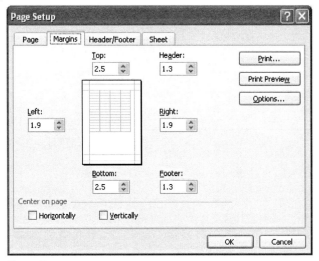

Figure 46

1. The Margins tab in the Page Setup option allows you to change the default settings Top, Bottom, Left, Right

2. The Header and Footer distances can also be changed from this screen

3. Click on the Horizontally and/or Vertically option to centre on the page

Header/Footer Option

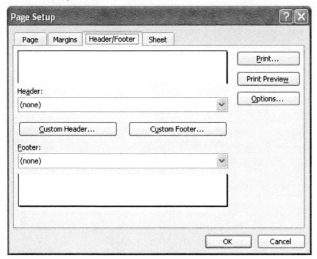

Figure 47

1. The He**a**der and **F**ooter area has a preview of both areas

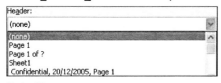

Figure 48

2. Choose the downward pointing arrows to view the standard preset options

3. The preview area displays the selected option

4. To create your Custom Header, select the [**C**ustom Header...] icon

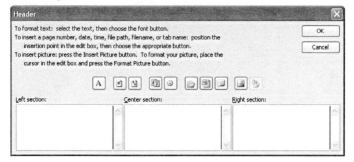

Figure 49

Header and Footer Toolbar Options	
Icon	**Descriptive Prompt**
A	Define font size and style options
	Inserts the Page Number
	Inserts Number of Pages
	Insert Date
	Insert Time
	File and Path
	Filename
	Tab Name
	Picture
	Format Picture Options
OK	Accept Changes and go back to Page Setup options
Cancel	Go back to the Page Set Up Options

Figure 50

5. The Header and Footer icons are those shown above

6. Create your Header and Footer information

7. The ⬚ Custom Footer... ⬚ icon enables the Footer area to be amended

8. Select ⬚ OK ⬚ twice to take you back to the preview area

9. Click ⬚ Close ⬚ to return to the worksheet

Exercise 4: - Creating Header and Footer Information

1. Open the workbook named Working with different formulas.xls
2. Go to the Header and Footer tab
3. Select the Custom Header
4. In the Centre section type the name of your organisation
5. Select the Custom Footer
6. In the Centre section create Page 1 of 1
7. Preview your worksheet to view the changes
8. Save the Workbook

Sheet Tab

The Sheet tab enables a print area to be selected within the worksheet.

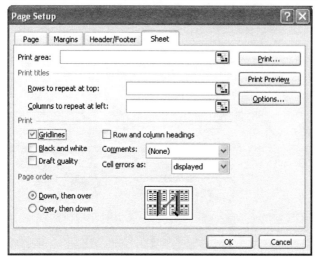

Figure 51

Define a Print Area

1. Select File, Page Setup

2. Select the Sheet tab

3. Click on the Print area icon

4. The Excel worksheet is displayed

Figure 52

5. Highlight the cells you want to print

6. The absolute references will appear in the print area

7. A dotted line appears around the selected area

8. Click on the icon to close the print area window

9. Click OK to close the Page Setup dialog box

10. Select File, Print

Clear Print Area

To clear a set print area.

1. Select File
2. Choose Print Area

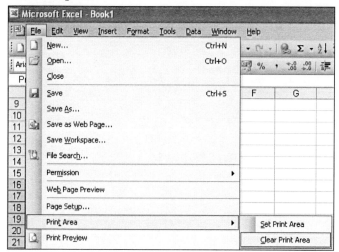

Figure 53

3. Select Clear Print Area

Print Preview

1. Select File, [Print Preview]
2. Alternatively select the Print Preview icon on the Standard Toolbar
3. Click on the [Zoom] icon to Zoom in or Zoom out of a page
4. If the mouse pointer is moved onto a page a magnifying glass appears
5. Click with the left button to zoom in and out of a page
6. [Next] and [Previous] displays the next or previous page
7. Hold down the left button, drag the vertical scroll bar to move between pages
8. The Status Bar area displays the page [Preview: Page 1 of 3] being viewed
9. Click on the [Margins] icon, to display or adjust the margins in the sheet
10. Select [Print...] to open the print dialog box

Spelling Check

1. Choose **T**ools, [🔤 **S**pelling...   F7]

2. Alternatively press [F7]

Printing

1. Select **F**ile, **P**rint
2. The print dialog box appears
3. The printer is defined
4. Click on the Na**m**e dialogue arrow to change the printer
5. Select the Print range required
6. Choose the Number of **c**opies required, default is 1 copy
7. Tick Collate to collate the worksheets
8. Select Acti**v**e Sheet(s)
9. Select the **E**ntire workbook if required
10. Click [Preview] to check the worksheet before printing
11. Select [OK]
12. Alternatively press the Print 🖨 icon on the Standard Toolbar to print

Introduction to Simple Charts

Excel allows you to create a chart from information that you have been working with and displays this data graphically in an embedded chart that can be placed and saved on the same sheet as your data, or on a chart sheet that displays the data separately from the data sheet. Both the embedded chart and the chart sheet are automatically updated when data on the worksheet is changed.

Different Parts of a Chart

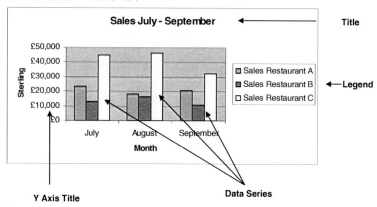

Figure 54

Chart Title

The chart title identifies the name of the chart.

Legend

The Legend defines the symbols used in each data series in the chart.

Y Axis Title

Indicates the unit of measurement used in the chart.

X Axis Title

Indicates the categories used in the chart.

Data Series

The Data Series represents a group of data incorporated in a row or column from an Excel worksheet. A chart consists of one or more data series.

A chart can be resized using the mouse by dragging from any of the corner points of the chart.

Creating a Simple Chart

1. Create the following table

	A	B	C	D	E	F
1		July	August	September	October	Total
2	Sales Restaurant A	£23,400	£18,200	£20,421	£15,876	£77,897
3	Sales Restaurant B	£13,275	£16,320	£10,745	£20,486	£60,826
4	Sales Restaurant C	£44,739	£46,100	£32,400	£30,200	£153,439

Figure 55

2. Select Cells A1 to D4 using the left button

3. Select Insert, ⬛ Chart... , Step 1 of the Chart Wizard appears

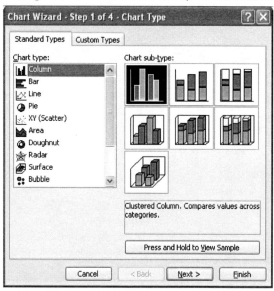

Figure 56

4. Select Standard Types, choose ⌷Clustered column with a 3-D visual effect.⌷

5. To view how the chart will look, click [Press and Hold to View Sample]

6. Press [Next >], Step 2 of the Chart Wizard appears

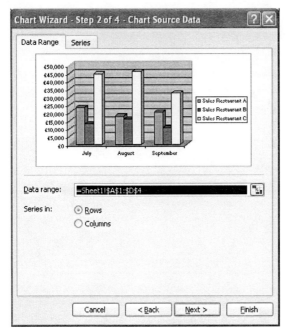

Figure 57

7. To add or remove data from the chart select the Series tab

8. Select ⬚Next >⬚ to proceed to Step 3 of Chart Wizard

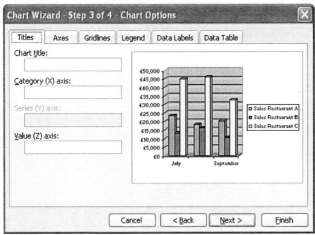

Figure 58

9. The Titles tab is highlighted

10. Type out the Chart <u>t</u>itle "Sales July to September"

11. Type "Months" in the <u>C</u>ategory (X) axis

12. Select the Gridlines tab to add or remove gridlines

13. The preview area displays the results in the Chart Wizard

14. Change where the legend appears by selecting the Legend tab

15. Choose [Next >]

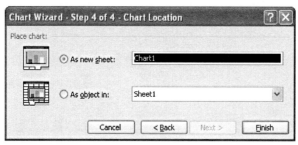

Figure 59

16. Click on As new <u>s</u>heet

17. Select [<u>F</u>inish] Chart 1 is displayed

18. Save the chart as My Simple Chart.xls

Adding New Data to a Chart

1. Click back into Sheet 1, the original data is displayed

2. In Column E the figures for October need to be added to the chart

3. Select cells E1 to E4 with the left button to highlight the cells

E
October
£15,876
£20,486
£30,200

Figure 60

4. Press the Copy 🗎 icon, select Chart 1, click on the Paste 🗎▾ icon

5. The new data for October is displayed in the chart

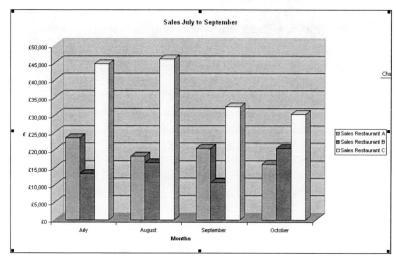

Figure 61

Printing a Chart Sheet

1. Click with the left button to select the chart, choose File, Print Preview

2. Select Setup... to change the orientation or scaling

3. The Margins tab allows margins to be altered and information centred

4. Select the Header/Footer tab

5. To create a Custom Header... or Custom Footer... select these tabs

6. To alter the chart size and quality select the Chart tab

7. Click OK to accept any changes, click Print..., OK

8. Save the workbook

Exercise 5: - Create a Chart within a Worksheet

Using the data in the previous section "Creating a Simple Chart", create a chart within a worksheet using the Chart Wizard

1. Alter the chart title to read "Restaurant Sales July to October"
2. Expand the chart area to display all the information
3. Print the chart including the original data
4. Save the workbook

Section 2: Intermediate Level Objectives

- Naming a Worksheet and Navigation

- Analysing Information in different Worksheets

- Working with Multiple Sheets

- Generate 3-D Formula

- Freezing Panes and Split Windows

- Working with Different Charts

- Vertical and Horizontal Lookup Functions

- Inserting Comments

- Password Protection

- Filtering Data

Naming a Worksheet and Navigation

Excel opens three worksheets in a workbook by default. To open more worksheets:

1. Choose **T**ools, **O**ptions, select the General tab

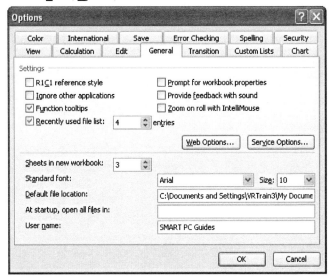

Figure 62

2. Change the **S**heets in new workbook from 3 to 5

3. Click 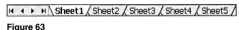 OK

4. The default is now changed to 5 sheets in any new workbooks

Note: **The number of worksheets is not changed in the current workbook but when a new workbook is selected the default is changed to 5.**

Inserting Worksheets

1. Open a new workbook to bring up the 5 sheets

`|◄ ◄ ► ►|` \ **Sheet1** / Sheet2 / Sheet3 / Sheet4 / Sheet5 /

Figure 63

2. Press Ctrl and Page Down to move through the sheets

3. The new active sheet appears to the right of the previously selected sheet

4. Select Ctrl and Page Up to move back a sheet

To View Unseen Worksheets

If worksheets are not displayed

1. Select the ⏮ icon with the left button to display sheet 1
2. Choose the ⏭ icon to display the last sheet in the workbook
3. Click the ◀ ▶ icons to display the concealed worksheets

Note: **The buttons will only show the name of the sheet, to activate the sheet click on the sheet.**

To View Sheet Tabs

1. Using the horizontal scroll bar
2. Move the mouse pointer over the left hand side of the arrow ◀
3. A black vertical double line appears with arrows each side of the lines
4. Click and hold down the left button and drag to the right
5. The concealed worksheets are displayed

To Rename a Sheet

1. Double click with the left button on sheet 1
2. The sheet name is highlighted Sheet1
3. Type the new name for the sheet, maximum of 31 characters

Rename a Sheet using the Right Mouse Button

1. Move the white arrow over sheet 2

Figure 64

2. Press the right button, select   Rename
3. The sheet is highlighted Sheet2
4. Rename the sheet as required
5. Press Enter, the new name is displayed

To Move a Sheet

1. Click and hold down the left 🖱 button on the required sheet

| ◄ ◄ ► ► |\ **Sheet1** / Sheet2 / Sheet3 / Sheet4 / Sheet5 /

Figure 65

2. A downward pointing black arrow appears on the sheet tab

3. Hold down the left 🖱 button, use the arrow as a guide

4. This displays where the new sheet will be positioned

5. Drag sheet 1 to its new position after sheet 3

6. Let go of the left 🖱 button, the sheet has moved to its new position

7. Move sheet 1 back to its original position

Move or Copy a Sheet

1. Select the sheet tab to be used using the left 🖱 button

2. Click with the right 🖱 button, select | Move or Copy... |

Figure 66

3. Select the location where the selected sheet needs to be moved

4. To create a copy, click with the left 🖱 button, choose ☑ Create a copy

5. Click | OK |

Note: To move or copy a new workbook or an active workbook that is opened select the ⌄ arrow in the To book: area.

To Move Sheets using the Menu Bar

1. Select the sheet tab to be moved
2. Click **E**dit, **M**ove or Copy Sheet

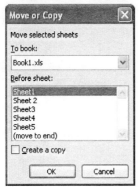

Figure 67

3. Select the appropriate location
4. Click OK

Applying Colours to Sheet Tabs

1. Select a sheet tab
2. Click with the right button, choose   Tab Color...

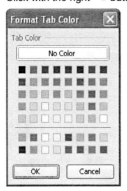

Figure 68

3. Select a colour, press   OK
4. The chosen colour is displayed under the sheet tab name Sheet3
5. Select a different tab, the full tab colour Sheet3 is displayed

Working with Multiple Sheets

Excel allows a number of sheets to be selected using the left 🖱 button. If you are creating a number of sheets using the same headings, highlight the sheets concerned, type the headings. The formatting will be applied to all the selected sheets.

1. Click on the tab named sheet 1

2. Hold down the `Ctrl` key and click on sheet 3 and sheet 5

3. When sheet 3 is selected the title bar displays **[Group]**

4. The word group identifies that more than one sheet is selected

5. Type in cell A1 SMART PC Guides

6. Widen column A

7. To deselect the group option

8. Click with the left 🖱 button on any sheet name that is not grouped

9. The group name disappears

10. SMART PC Guides appears on sheets 1, 3 and 5

Note: **To select a group of sheets next to each other, click on the first sheet, select `Shift` before clicking on the last sheet. All the sheets are selected and the Title Bar displays the Group option.**

To Delete Sheets

1. Click with the right 🖱 button over the sheet tab to be deleted

2. Select `Delete`

3. The sheet is deleted from the workbook

To Print Multiple Sheets

1. Select the sheets that require printing

2. The **[Group]** selection is displayed in the Title Bar

3. Click <u>F</u>ile, <u>P</u>rint to display the Print dialog box

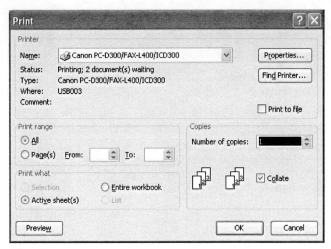

Figure 69

4. Choose Acti*ve* sheet(s)

5. Select [Previe*w*]

6. Press the [Next] and [Previous] icons to display the workbooks

7. To change the layout of a page select the [Setup...] icon

8. Select Print to print the sheets

Exercise 6: - Working with Multiple Sheets

1. Click with the left 🖱 button on 🗔 New Workbook
2. Rename four worksheets Qtr 1, Qtr 2, Qtr 3, Qtr 4
3. Group Sheets Qtr 1 to Qtr 4
4. Create the information below
5. Format cells B2:E5, Column F and Row 7 to Currency
6. Use AutoSum to create the totals

	A	B	C	D	E	F
1		North	South	East	West	Total
2	Company 1					£0
3	Company 2					£0
4	Company 3					£0
5	Company 4					£0
6						£0
7	Total	£0	£0	£0	£0	

7. Ungroup all the sheets
8. Select the sheet named Qtr 1
9. Create a copy of Qtr 1, rename the Sheet Consolidation
10. In Qtr 1 type the following data

	A	B	C	D	E	F
1		North	South	East	West	Total
2	Company 1	£14,000	£86,000	£74,000	£89,000	£263,000
3	Company 2	£73,000	£89,000	£55,000	£23,000	£240,000
4	Company 3	£46,000	£29,000	£67,000	£15,000	£157,000
5	Company 4	£8,000	£43,000	£23,000	£18,000	£92,000
6						
7	Total	£141,000	£247,000	£219,000	£145,000	

11. In Qtr 2 type the following data

	A	B	C	D	E	F
1		North	South	East	West	Total
2	Company 1	£14,000	£7,000	£21,000	£20,000	£62,000
3	Company 2	£23,000	£11,000	£12,000	£10,000	£56,000
4	Company 3	£22,000	£46,000	£46,000	£46,000	£160,000
5	Company 4	£8,000	£8,000	£8,000	£8,000	£32,000
6						
7	Total	£67,000	£72,000	£87,000	£84,000	

12. In Qtr 3 type the following data

	A	B	C	D	E	F
1		North	South	East	West	Total
2	Company 1	£120,000	£86,000	£43,000	£28,000	£277,000
3	Company 2	£23,000	£132,000	£54,000	£45,000	£254,000
4	Company 3	£46,000	£120,000	£12,000	£33,000	£211,000
5	Company 4	£32,000	£8,000	£8,000	£8,000	£56,000
6						
7	Total	£221,000	£346,000	£117,000	£114,000	

13. Type the following data for Qtr 4

	A	B	C	D	E	F
1		North	South	East	West	Total
2	Company 1	£14,000	£14,000	£76,000	£14,000	£118,000
3	Company 2	£23,000	£122,000	£23,000	£23,000	£191,000
4	Company 3	£46,000	£18,000	£32,000	£63,000	£159,000
5	Company 4	£38,000	£12,000	£56,000	£83,000	£189,000
6						
7	Total	£121,000	£166,000	£187,000	£183,000	

14. Save the workbook as Working with Multiple Sheets.xls

Creating 3 Dimensional Formula

To analyse data in the same cell or range of cells on multiple worksheets, it is possible to create a 3D formula.

1. Open Working with Multiple Sheets.xls
2. Select the Consolidation worksheet, choose cell B2
3. To create a 3D formula Type =sum(
4. Click on worksheet Quarter 1
5. Hold the ⎡Shift⎤ key down, select worksheet Quarter 4
6. Select cell B2
7. The formula is displayed in the formula bar ⎡=sum('Qtr 1:Qtr 4'!B2⎤
8. Click on the green tick ☑ to confirm the formula
9. The result is displayed in cell B2 in the Consolidation Worksheet
10. Use the black cross Fill Handle to drag down to cell E5
11. The formula has added up the data in cell B2 in each quarter
12. Save to update the workbook

Note: **If a worksheet is moved or inserted into a workbook that contains a 3D formula, the formula incorporates the figures in the results of the formula. The opposite is true if a sheet was part of a 3D formula and the sheet was moved or deleted.**

Window Panes

Excel can freeze a column that will enable the heading rows to be seen at all times as you scroll across a worksheet.

Freeze Left Pane

1. Open Working with Multiple Sheets.xls
2. Choose worksheet Quarter 4
3. Select cell B2
4. Click on **W**indow, **F**reeze Panes
5. Black indicator lines appear both to the left and above cell B2
6. Using the ⬛ key move along the row
7. The Heading rows are visible as you move to cell Z2
8. To move back a cell at a time use the ⬛ key
9. Freeze panes ensures both column and row headings are visible
10. To unfreeze panes, choose **W**indow Un**f**reeze Panes

Note: **Using Freeze Panes does not change or affect the printing of a worksheet.**

To Freeze the Top Pane

1. Select cell A2, the row below the Column Headings
2. Click on **W**indow, **F**reeze Panes
3. A Horizontal freeze pane line appears throughout the workbook
4. Use the ⬛ to go to cell A75, all the column headings remain
5. Unfreeze the pane
6. Press Save

Splitting a Window View

Splitting a window enables a user to view different areas of a large worksheet at the same time. The screen can be split into four different sections.

1. Place the cursor where you want the split to appear
2. Select **W**indow, **S**plit
3. The screen splits into four sections
4. To move a split
5. Move the mouse pointer over the split line
6. Press and hold down the left ⬛ button, drag to the required position
7. To remove the split screen select **W**indow, Remove **S**plit

Working with Different Chart Types

Different Charts allows information to be easily understood by evaluating data and making it more interesting to read. Charts can also be used to help analyse and compare data.

Creating a Cylinder Chart

1. Create the following information below

	A	B	C	D	E	F
1		July	August	September	October	Total
2	A	£23,400	£18,200	£20,421	£18,876	£80,897
3	B	£13,275	£16,320	£10,745	£20,486	£60,826
4	C	£44,739	£46,100	£32,400	£30,200	£153,439

Figure 70

2. Save the worksheet as Working with Charts.xls

3. Select Cell A1:D4, choose the Chart Wizard 📊 icon

4. Step 1 of the Chart Wizard appears

5. Select **C**hart type and choose 🛢 Cylinder

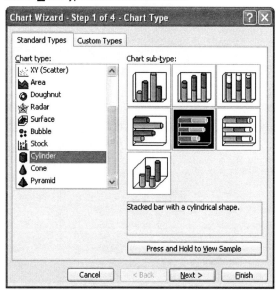

Figure 71

6. Select the Stacked bar with a cylindrical shape icon

7. Press with the left 🖑 button on ⬚ Press and Hold to View Sample

8. This displays a preview of how the chart will appear, click Next >

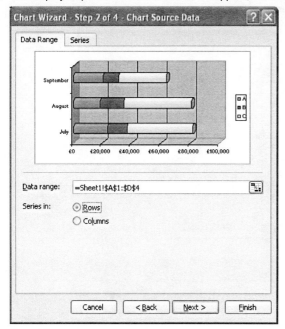

Figure 72

9. In the Data Range tab, change the Series to ⊙ Columns

10. Select Next > to proceed to Step 3, choose Titles

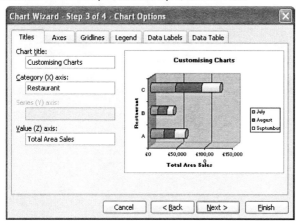

Figure 73

11. Complete Chart title, **C**ategory (X) axis and **V**alue (Z) axis as above

12. Select the Legend tab

13. Click ⊙ Bottom to place the legend at the bottom area of the chart

14. Select Next > to progress to Step 4

Figure 74

15. Choose new **s**heet, press Finish

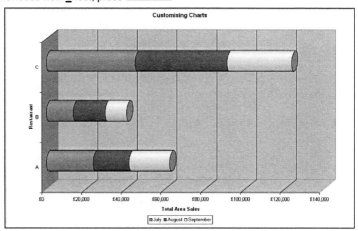

Figure 75

16. The Chart is displayed on a new sheet

Customising the Chart

1. Move the mouse pointer over the September series

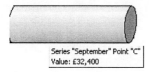

Series "September" Point "C"
Value: £32,400

Figure 76

2. Click with the left 🖱 button once in the September Series Restaurant C

3. The September Series for restaurants A, B and C are highlighted

4. Click again with the left 🖱 button in September Series Restaurant C

Figure 77

5. Restaurant C for September is now highlighted

6. Click with the Right 🖱 button over the area choose [📄 Format Data Point...]

7. The Format Data Point dialog box appears

8. Select [Data Labels], click with the left 🖱 button in the [☑ Series name]

9. Press [OK]

10. The Series name appears only in Restaurant C

September

Figure 78

11. Repeat the process, for Restaurant A to display the **V**alue option

12. Choose the **C**ategory name option to be displayed for Restaurant B

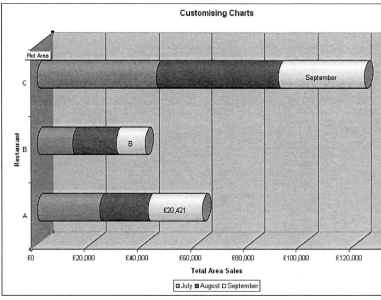

Figure 79

13. Double click with the left 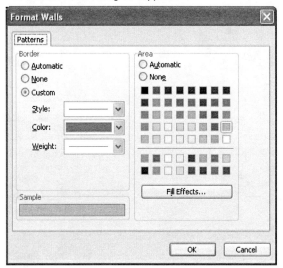 button in the background wall area

14. The Format Walls dialog box appears

Figure 80

15. Select

16. Choose [Gradient] tab, click two colours

17. Set two different colours, select a shading style

18. Click [OK] twice

Customising Charts

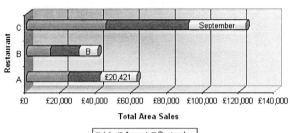

Figure 81

19. Repeat the process to define a floor shaded area

Adding Additional Data to a Chart

1. Select the sheet containing the original data

2. Highlight Cells E1:E4 for the month of October

3. Press **E**dit, [⎙ Copy   Ctrl+C]

4. Click on Chart 1

5. Select **E**dit, [⎙ Paste   Ctrl+V]

6. The data for October appears in the chart

Note: If the chart and data appear on the same worksheet, highlight the data and drag onto the chart.

Add Data Table Information

1. Click with the left ⌐🖰 button to select the chart

2. Select the Chart [📊] icon

3. Proceed to Step 3 of the Chart Wizard

4. Select the [Data Table] tab

5. Place a tick in [☑ Show data table]

6. Deselect Show **l**egend keys option

7. Press [Finish]

8. The table data information is displayed in the chart

	A	B	C
October	£18,876	£20,486	£30,200
September	£20,421	£10,745	£32,400
August	£18,200	£16,320	£46,100
July	£23,400	£13,275	£44,739

Figure 82

Changing the Table Series Order

1. Double click in Restaurant C Series
2. The Format Data Series dialog box appears

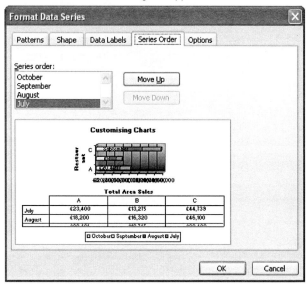

Figure 83

3. Select Series Order
4. Highlight October
5. Click with the left button on the `Move Down` or `Move Up` icons
6. This will adjust the chart order of the data
7. Repeat the process for the remaining months
8. Click `OK`
9. The updated data appears in the table

Changing the Shape of the Data Series

1. Double click with the left 🖱 button in Restaurant C Series
2. The Format Data Series dialog box appears
3. Select the ⌐Shape⌐ tab

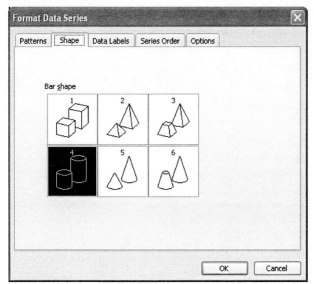

Figure 84

4. Select Bar shape 1
5. Click ⌐ OK ⌐
6. The chart changes to the selected new shape
7. Save the workbook

Changing the Chart Style

1. Click with the right button on the white background in the chart area

Figure 85

2. Select [Chart Type...]

3. Choose Chart Type: Column, Chart sub-type: 3-D Column

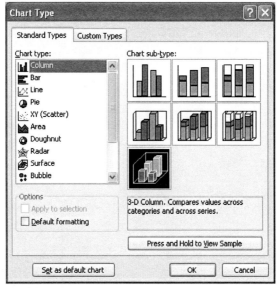

Figure 86

4. Click [OK],the new chart style is displayed

Changing the 3-D View

1. Move the Mouse pointer over the back wall of the chart
2. Press the right button on the wall of the chart
3. Select 3-D **V**iew

Figure 87

4. The following dialog box appears when a 3D chart is displayed

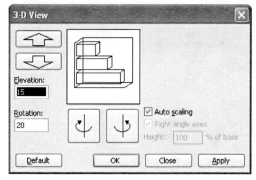

Figure 88

5. Change the Elevation using the ⬆ and ⬇ arrows
6. Alter the Rotation using the rotation arrows
7. Select Apply
8. Click Close to return to display the chart

Create a User Defined Chart

1. Click outside the chart area

2. Press the right 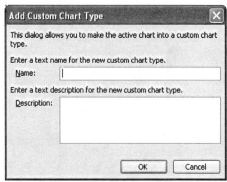 button, select, [Chart Type...]

3. Choose the [Custom Types] tab

> Select from
> ○ User-defined
> ⊙ Built-in

Figure 89

4. Choose [⊙ User-defined]

5. Click [Add...]

6. The Add Custom Chart Type dialog box appears

> **Add Custom Chart Type**   ☒
>
> This dialog allows you to make the active chart into a custom chart type.
>
> Enter a text name for the new custom chart type.
> Name: | I |
>
> Enter a text description for the new custom chart type.
> Description:
>
> [OK]   [Cancel]

Figure 90

7. Create a Name for the Custom Chart and a description

8. Press [OK] twice to return to the Excel worksheet

Interpreting Data in Charts

Charts can show the same data but in a different format. The data can be interpreted in different ways.

1. Open the workbook Working with Charts.xls

2. Click with the right 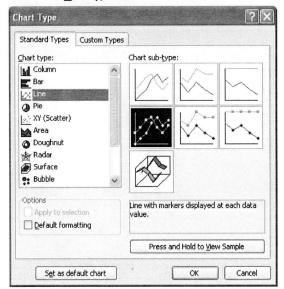 button outside the chart area

3. Choose the **C**hart type: Line

Figure 91

4. Press [OK]

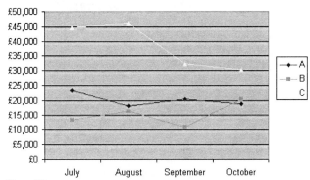

Figure 92

Note: **When the mouse pointer is moved over a marker, the individual data is displayed.**

Displaying Data in a Different Format

1. Move the mouse pointer 🕱 in the chart area

2. Press the right 🖰 button, select **C**hart type:

3. Select the line chart displayed below

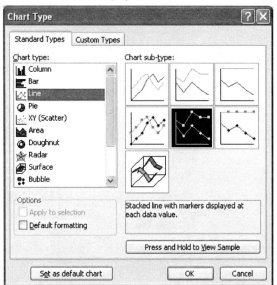

Figure 93

4. Click [OK]

5. Save and close the workbook

Note: The chart represents the running total monthly figures as displayed on the Y axis.

Vertical and Horizontal Lookup Functions

The Lookup functions can be used to locate data in a selected table, database or list. Vertical Lookup (VLOOKUP) searches for a value in the left most column of a table and then returns a value in the same row from a column that has been specified in the table, database or list. Horizontal Lookup (HLOOKUP) searches for a value in the top row of the table, database or list and returns a value in the same column from a row that has been specified.

Vertical Lookup

1. Click on a New Worksheet

2. Generate the following information

	A	B	C	D	E
1					
2		Sales Volume £			
3	Name	2000	2001	2002	2003
4	Roger Ainsworth	£26,000	£26,950	£27,360	£27,750
5	Derek Bowen	£25,958	£26,925	£27,275	£27,800
6	Rachel James	£27,200	£26,970	£26,575	£27,100
7	Jeff Robson	£25,300	£26,100	£26,900	£27,000
8	Andy Scott	£26,000	£26,750	£27,150	£27,250
9	Burt Thomson	£27,900	£28,360	£28,956	£28,755
10	Lesley Turnbull	£25,320	£25,950	£26,300	£26,900
11	Donna Varney	£26,970	£27,110	£27,150	£27,390
12	Daniel Williams	£27,500	£26,100	£27,350	£27,735

Figure 94

3. Create the tabled information below to use in the vlookup formula

	A	B
22	Commission Payments	
23	£25,000	1.00%
24	£25,500	1.50%
25	£26,000	2.00%
26	£26,500	2.50%
27	£27,000	3.00%
28	£27,500	3.50%
29	£28,000	4.00%
30	£28,500	4.50%

Figure 95

4. Highlight cells A22:B30

5. Select Insert, Name, Define

6. The Define Name dialog box appears

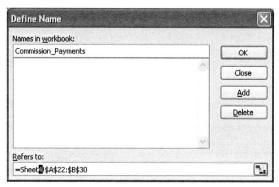

Figure 96

7. Select ⬚ Add ⬚, choose ⬚ OK ⬚

8. Press ⬚F5⬚, highlight Commission Payments

9. Click ⬚ OK ⬚

10. The corresponding table is highlighted

11. Create the following information in cells A16 and A18

	A	B	C	D	E
16	Roger Ainsworth				
17					
18	Donna Varney				
19					

Figure 97

12. To create a vlookup formula, for quarterly commission payments as a %

13. Click in cell B16

14. Type **=vlookup(B4,Commission_Payments,2)**, press ⬚Enter⬚

Note: **B4 in the formula represents Roger Ainsworth's Sales volume for the year 2000, Commission_Payments represents the named area used in the formula and the number 2 instructs the formula to look at the information in column 2.**

15. The result is 2% in cell B16

16. Click in cell B16, use the Black Fill Handle to drag to E16

17. Format the cells into a percentage format

18. To calculate the formula as a £ value

19. Select cell B17 type =B4*B16 to calculate the amount of commission

20. This represents 26000 multiplied by 2%

21. Drag the relative formula to cell E17

22. Follow the steps to complete the information for Donna Varney

23. The results are outlined below

	A	B	C	D	E
16	Roger Ainsworth	2.0%	2.5%	3.0%	3.5%
17		£520.00	£673.75	£820.80	£971.25
18	Donna Varney	2.5%	3.0%	3.0%	3.0%
19		£674.25	£813.30	£814.50	£821.70

Figure 98

Using Horizontal Lookup

The formula for horizontal lookup is, select the column, select the table, select the row.

1. Open a new workbook

2. Create the following table, format the cells as shown below

	A	B	C	D	E	F	G	H
1	Name	January	February	March	April	May	June	Totals
2	Goods In	£5,890.00	£4,671.00	£5,891.00	£4,998.00	£3,297.00	£3,789.00	£28,536.00
3	Sewing	£7,902.00	£7,857.00	£7,985.00	£6,342.00	£6,876.00	£7,203.00	£44,165.00
4	Tooling	£9,230.00	£7,350.00	£6,892.00	£5,890.00	£6,003.00	£5,907.00	£41,272.00
5	Spraying	£9,890.00	£7,750.00	£5,999.00	£6,002.00	£7,090.00	£6,325.00	£43,056.00
6	Maintenance	£11,009.00	£12,340.00	£15,700.00	£11,786.00	£10,906.00	£10,870.00	£72,611.00
7	Despatch	£14,560.00	£16,900.00	£15,650.00	£14,340.00	£14,980.00	£16,987.00	£93,417.00
8	Material	£15,900.00	£16,723.00	£17,230.00	£16,800.00	£15,236.00	£14,009.00	£95,898.00
9	Export	£17,340.00	£17,551.00	£17,340.00	£16,996.00	£18,000.00	£17,909.00	£105,136.00
10	Totals	£91,721.00	£91,142.00	£92,687.00	£83,154.00	£82,388.00	£82,999.00	

Figure 99

3. Highlight cells A1 to H10

4. Select Insert, Name, Define, name the table as Production

5. Using hlookup create a table that displays

   a. The monthly costs for Goods In for the months of January and May

   b. The results for January and May Goods In are £5,890 and £3,297

	A	B	C
28		January	May
29	Goods In	=hlookup(b1,production,2)	=hlookup(f1,production,2)

Figure 100

6. Save the workbook as Using Horizontal Lookup

Note: **Unlike vlookup, hlookup formulas are created individually. Displayed above is the result for January Goods In & May Goods In, the word "production" relates to the defined area A1:H10.**

Exercise: - 7 Using Horizontal Lookup

1. Open the workbook Using Horizontal Lookup.xls

2. Using hlookup update the table to include

   a. The monthly costs for Despatch and Export for the months of January and May

   b. The Total costs for Goods In, Despatch and Export

	A	B	C	D
28		January	May	Totals
29	Goods In	£5,890	£3,297	
30	Despatch			
31	Export			

3. Save the workbook

Working with Comments

Excel allows you to insert comments to a cell that can easily be viewed or printed.

Insert Comments

1. Open an existing workbook
2. Click in a cell
3. Select Insert,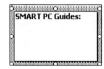
4. A comments box appears

SMART PC Guides:

Figure 101

5. Type the required text
6. Click outside the comment to deselect
7. Select Tools,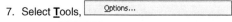
8. Choose View
9. Click Comment indicator only

Figure 102

10. Press OK
11. A red marker appears in the cell containing the comment

To View a Comment

1. Move the cursor into the cell containing the comment
2. The comments box appears
3. To deselect, move the curser outside the cell
4. Alternatively press F5, choose Special...
5. The Go To Special dialog box appears

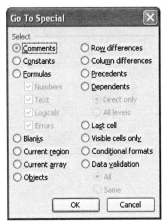

Figure 103

6. Select **C**omments and click

7. All the cells containing comments are highlighted

8. To view any comment move the mouse pointer over the highlighted cell

Edit a Comment

1. Select **V**iew, **T**oolbars, | Reviewing |

2. The Reviewing Toolbar appears

Figure 104

3. Click in the cell that contains a comment

4. The icons change when you click in a cell that contains a comment

Reviewing

Figure 105

5. Click on the Edit Comment 📝 icon

6. Amend the comment, then click back in the cell with the edited comment

7. The edited comment is displayed

To Delete a Comment

1. Select the cell, click on the delete 🗑 icon on the Reviewing Toolbar

2. The comment is deleted from the cell

To Show All Comments in a Worksheet

1. Click on the Show All Comments ▣ icon
2. Select the same icon to Hide All Comments

To Move a Comments Box

1. Click in the cell
2. Position the cursor over the edge of the comments box
3. Click with the left ✎ button, drag to the new location

To Adjust the Size of the Comments Box

1. Click in the cell
2. Position the cursor over the edge of the comments box
3. Press the left ✎ button
4. Using the resizing handles drag to the new size

To Print Comments

1. Select File, Page Setup, Sheet

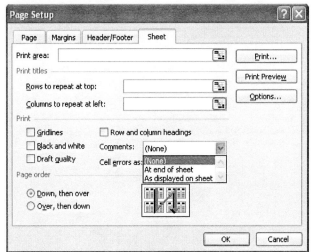

Figure 106

2. In the Comments area, Select At end of sheet
3. Alternatively select As displayed on sheet
4. Click OK , press Print Preview
5. Choose Next to display the comments
6. Press Print... or Close to return to the Worksheet

Password Protection

Excel provides several ways to restrict access to a workbook by assigning a password. **PASSWORD, WRITE IT DOWN AND KEEP IT SAFE. If you lose the password, you cannot open or gain access to the data in the password protected workbook**.

Protecting a Workbook

1. Open a Workbook

2. Select File, Save As

3. Select Tools ▾ , General Options...

4. The Save Options dialog box appears

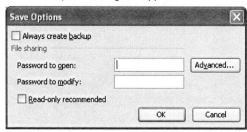

Figure 107

5. Passwords are case sensitive and up to 15 characters long

6. In the Password to open box type in a password of your choice

7. Press OK

Figure 108

8. Re-enter the password, click OK

9. Save the Workbook

10. Enter the password to re-opened the workbook

11. Click OK

To Change a Password

1. Open a Workbook
2. Select File, Save As
3. Select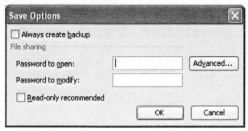
4. The Save Options dialog box appears

Figure 109

5. Select Password to modify, type in the new password
6. Click OK
7. Retype the password

Figure 110

8. Click OK
9. Save the workbook

To Remove a Password

1. Open a Workbook
2. Select File, Save As
3. Select Tools ▼, General Options...
4. The Save Options dialog box appears

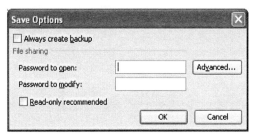

Figure 111

5. Delete the password, click [OK]

6. Save the workbook

7. A prompt asks "Do you want to replace the existing file?"

8. Click [Yes]

Protecting a Sheet

1. Open a Workbook

2. Select **T**ools, **P**rotection, [🔒 **P**rotect Sheet...]

3. The Protect Sheet dialog box appears

Figure 112

4. Click, [OK]

5. Alternatively type a password, **R**e-enter password again

6. Press [OK]

Protecting a Range

1. Open Exercise 7 Using Horizontal Lookup.xls

	B	C	D	E	F	G	H
1	January	February	March	April	May	June	Totals
2	£5,890.00	£4,671.00	£5,891.00	£4,998.00	£3,297.00	£3,789.00	£28,536.00
3	£7,902.00	£7,857.00	£7,985.00	£6,342.00	£6,876.00	£7,203.00	£44,165.00
4	£9,230.00	£7,350.00	£6,892.00	£5,890.00	£6,003.00	£5,907.00	£41,272.00
5	£9,890.00	£7,750.00	£5,999.00	£6,002.00	£7,090.00	£6,325.00	£43,056.00
6	£11,009.00	£12,340.00	£15,700.00	£11,786.00	£10,906.00	£10,870.00	£72,611.00
7	£14,560.00	£16,900.00	£15,650.00	£14,340.00	£14,980.00	£16,987.00	£93,417.00
8	£15,900.00	£16,723.00	£17,230.00	£16,800.00	£15,236.00	£14,009.00	£95,898.00
9	£17,340.00	£17,551.00	£17,340.00	£16,996.00	£18,000.00	£17,909.00	£105,136.00
10	£91,721.00	£91,142.00	£92,687.00	£83,154.00	£82,388.00	£82,999.00	

Figure 113

2. Select **T**ools, **P**rotection, Allow Users to Edit Ranges…

3. The following dialog box appears

Figure 114

4. Select **N**ew, the New Range dialog box appears

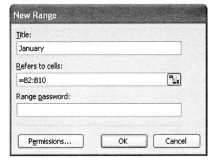

Figure 115

5. Type January in the Title area

6. Select 🔲 in the refer to cells area

7. Select cells B2:B10

8. Click 🔲 to confirm the range

9. In the Range password area, type January

10. Click ⟨ OK ⟩, re-enter the password

11. Select ⟨ OK ⟩

12. Repeat the process for February using the password February

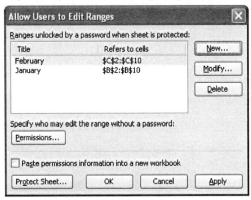

Figure 116

13. Select ⟨ Protect Sheet... ⟩, click ⟨ OK ⟩

14. Save the worksheet

15. Click in cell F5 and try to change the data in this cell

16. The following prompt appears

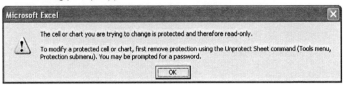

Figure 117

17. Alternatively double click in cell B8, the following dialog box appears

Figure 118

18. Enter January in the password area

19. Click [OK]

20. Amendments to the selected range can now be made

21. Save and close the workbook

Filtering Data

Sorting and filtering large amounts of data within a worksheet using the AutoFilter and Advanced Filter allows new data to be displayed as a sub-section view.

Sorting and Filtering Data

Location	Section	Surname	First Name	DOB	Start Date	Job Title	Salary
Leeds	HR	Roberts	Samuel	09/03/1954	27/03/1976	HR Officer	£33,276
Newark	Logistics	Gillespie	Nicola	08/01/1957	09/08/1989	Manager	£18,230
Leicester	Payroll	Davies	Terry	08/02/1958	02/01/1988	Payroll Clerk	£13,250
Leicester	Logistics	Collins	Laura	16/06/1963	11/10/2000	Traffic Admin	£16,570
Leeds	HR	Lesley	David	14/07/1963	12/12/1985	HR Officer	£32,950
Barnsley	Accounts	Gillian	Diana	13/10/1967	15/07/1990	Cost Clerk	£11,357
Derby	HR	Payne	Barry	21/10/1970	07/12/2000	HR Manager	£29,950
Grantham	Accounts	Andrews	Colin	26/03/1972	01/01/1992	Clerk	£13,760
Rotherham	Training	Rogers	Rachel	16/01/1976	01/10/1991	Training Mgr	£27,950
Derby	IT	Cobb	Jane	05/05/1976	29/09/1996	Consultant	£27,350
Leeds	Buying	Smith	Melanie	27/11/1981	19/08/2001	Buying Clerk	£8,100
Sheffield	Marketing	Hopkins	James	08/04/1983	03/06/2003	Clerk	£15,600
Grantham	Buying	Buckley	Christopher	17/07/1984	01/01/2000	Buyer	£25,250
Barnsley	Payroll	Brooks	Thomas	12/08/1984	20/07/2002	Payroll Clerk	£8,950
Sheffield	IT	Murray	Phillip	10/07/1985	01/12/2002	Consultant	£27,350
Rotherham	IT	Bassett	Michael	09/07/1986	01/12/2002	Consultant	£30,205
Mansfield	Cust Care	Vale	Andrew	13/11/1987	19/04/2001	Care Clerk	£10,590

Figure 119

1. Open a blank **N**ew Workbook

2. Create the above data within a worksheet

3. Save the workbook as Sorting and Filtering Data.xls

4. Click in a cell that contains data

5. Select **D**ata,

6. The Sort dialog box appears

Figure 120

7. Select Location, choose **A**scending in the Sort by box

8. Select Section, **A**scending in the second box

9. Click **OK**

10. Generate a sort using the criteria, Section **A**scending, Job Title As**c**ending, Salary _Descendin**g**

11. Save the workbook

Using AutoFilter

1. Select a cell containing the list of data

2. Click, **D**ata, **F**ilter, AutoF**i**lter

3. In the headings a downward arrow indicates the filtering option

4. Click on the arrow in the heading **Section ▾**

5. Choose Buying

6. The arrow changes to blue when a filter is applied

7. The information displays members of staff in the Buying Section

8. Filtering hides all the rows that do not match the criteria

9. To cancel the filter click on the blue arrow and select All

Creating a Custom Filter

1. Click on the arrow in the heading [Salary ▼]

2. Select the option Custom

3. Complete the Custom AutoFilter as below

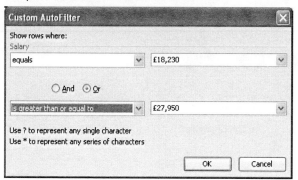

Figure 121

4. Press [OK]

5. The data is as follows

	A	B	C	D	E	F	G	H
1	Location ▼	Section ▼	Surname ▼	First Nan ▼	DOB ▼	Start Dat ▼	Job Title ▼	Salary ▼
7	Derby	HR	Payne	Barry	21/10/1970	07/12/2000	HR Manage	£29,950
8	Leeds	HR	Lesley	David	14/07/1963	12/12/1985	HR Officer	£32,950
9	Leeds	HR	Roberts	Samuel	09/03/1954	27/03/1976	HR Officer	£33,276
12	Rotherham	IT	Bassett	Michael	09/07/1986	01/12/2002	Consultant	£30,205
13	Newark	Logistics	Gillespie	Nicola	08/01/1957	09/08/1989	Manager	£18,230
18	Rotherham	Training	Rogers	Rachel	16/01/1976	01/10/1991	Training Mgr	£27,950

Figure 122

6. Create a custom filter of your choice based upon the salary data

Advanced Filter

The Advanced Filter is used to create more complex criteria to be filtered.

1. Using the workbook Sorting and Filtering Data.xls

2. Click in a blank cell beneath the main data

3. Type or copy the headings for the advanced filter as shown below

	A	B	C
23	Location	Salary	Salary
24	Rotherham	>=15000	
25	Leeds	>=18000	<=34000

Figure 123

4. In this instance the advanced filter has been asked to locate staff with salaries greater than or equal to £15,000 in Rotherham and salaries greater than or equal to £18,000 but less than or equal to £34,000 in Leeds

5. Click anywhere in the original data

6. Sort the location field into alphabetical order

7. Select **D**ata, **F**ilter ⌐ Advanced Filter... ⌐

8. The Advanced Filter Dialog box appears

Figure 124

9. A dotted line appears around the original data

10. In this example, click with the left 🖱 button to C**o**py to another location

11. Press ⌐ Tab ⌐, the original data is highlighted in the **L**ist range area

12. Select ⌐ Tab ⌐ to move to the **C**riteria range

13. Click the 🔲 icon to select the advanced criteria including the headings

14. Click the 🔲 icon to return to the Advanced Filter Dialog box

15. Press ⌐ Tab ⌐ to move to Copy **t**o

16. Click in cell A30

17. Choose ⌐ OK ⌐

18. The results are shown below

Location	Section	Surname	First Name	DOB	Start Date	Job Title	Salary
Leeds	HR	Lesley	David	14/07/1963	12/12/1985	HR Officer	£32,950
Leeds	HR	Roberts	Samuel	09/03/1954	27/03/1976	HR Officer	£33,276
Rotherham	IT	Bassett	Michael	09/07/1986	01/12/2002	Consultant	£30,205
Rotherham	Training	Rogers	Rachel	16/01/1976	01/10/1991	Training Mgr	£27,950

Figure 125

Exercise: 8 - Using the Advanced Filter

1. Open the workbook Sorting and Filtering Data.xls

2. Set the criteria to find Staff based in Barnsley and Leicester

3. Copy the Advanced filter to another location

4. The result shows four people that match the criteria

5. Select Data, Filter, Show All to return to the original data

6. Using the Advanced Filter, define the criteria to find Nicola Gillespie and Colin Andrews

7. Choose Filter the list, in-place

8. The results show the data on Nicola Gillespie and Colin Andrews

9. Select Data, Filter, Show All to return to the original data

10. Save the workbook

Using Data Form

1. Open the workbook Sorting and Filtering Data.xls

2. Click in the original data

3. Select **D**ata, F**o**rm

4. The data is displayed as below

Figure 126

5. The icons enable the user to add, delete and find information

6. Select Ne**w**

7. Create a New form using [Tab] or [Shift] [Tab] to move through the fields

8. Click [C**l**ose]

9. The new data appears in the last row of the data

10. The new data is not automatically sorted or placed in any previous advanced filter

11. Save and close the Workbook

Using the Subtotals feature

1. Open the workbook Sorting a Filtering Data.xls
2. Sort the Section area into alphabetical order
3. Select **D**ata, [Su**b**totals...]
4. The Subtotals dialog box appears
5. Select the following criteria

Figure 127

6. Click, [OK]
7. The results are shown below

1 2 3		A	B	C	D	E	F	G	H
	1	Location ▼	Section ▼	Surname ▼	First Nar ▼	DOB ▼	Start Dat ▼	Job Title ▼	Salary ▼
·	2	Barnsley	Accounts	Gillian	Diana	13/10/1967	15/07/1990	Cost Clerk	£11,357
·	3	Grantham	Accounts	Andrews	Colin	26/03/1972	01/01/1992	Clerk	£13,760
−	4		**Accounts Total**						£25,117
·	5	Leeds	Buying	Smith	Melanie	27/11/1981	19/08/2001	Buying Clerk	£8,100
·	6	Grantham	Buying	Buckley	Christopher	17/07/1984	01/01/2000	Buyer	£25,250
−	7		**Buying Total**						£33,350

Figure 128

8. There are 3 outline icons to the left of Column A [1 2 3]
9. Select 1 to display the grand total
10. Select 2 to display the Section Totals
11. Select 3 to display all the criteria

Removing Subtotals

1. Click in the original data
2. Select **D**ata, [Su**b**totals...], press [**R**emove All]

Section 3: Expert Level Objectives

- Creating Range Names

- Creating Range Labels

- Auditing a Worksheet

- Using Watch Window

- Strings and Text Functions

- Logical Functions

- Outlining a Worksheet

- Data Consolidation

- Templates

- Scenario Manager

- Custom Views

- Pivot Tables

- Macros

- What is XML?

Range Names

When working in Excel a cell or block of cells can be defined using meaningful names up to 255 characters long, for example =sum(A2:D2) can be defined as =Sum(Leeds: Leicester). Names can also be applied to formulas.

Advantages of Range Names

1. It is easier to remember a name rather than a cell reference
2. Formulas are easier to understand
3. When a name is redefined all formulas using the name are updated
4. Using Range Names makes navigation around a worksheet faster

Define a Range Name

1. Click with the left ⌂ button in a cell or select a range of cells
2. Select Insert, Name, Define
3. Alternatively press Ctrl F3 to display the Define Name box

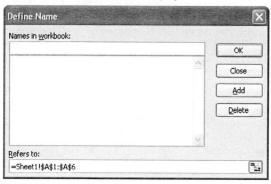

Figure 129

4. Define a specific name for the range of cells
5. Click Add
6. Choose OK
7. Click in any cell outside the selected range
8. Move the cursor to the Name Box area on the Formula Bar
9. Click the ▼ arrow, select the newly defined name
10. The range is highlighted

Delete a Defined Name

1. Select Insert, Name, Define or press Ctrl F3
2. Click with the left 🖰 button on the name to be deleted
3. Press Delete
4. Select OK

Creating a Range of Names

The create feature allows multiple names to be created in one instruction.

1. Create the following information

	A	B	C	D
1	**Newspaper Sales**	**Jan**	**Feb**	**Mar**
2	The Daily Telegraph	12090	13009	13090
3	The Mail	15102	15602	15765
4	The Guardian	11090	10358	10975
5	Financial Times	8759	9035	8950
6	Total	47041	48004	48780

Figure 130

2. Highlight cells A1:D5
3. Select Insert, Name, Create... , the Create Names dialog box appears

Figure 131

4. Select Top row and Left Column, click OK
5. Move the cursor to the Name Box area on the Formula Bar
6. Click the ▼ arrow, select "The Mail", the data is highlighted

Using the Apply Names Feature

If formulas have been used within the selected area before the names are applied then the formula names will not be displayed. In order for the formula to be displayed a name will need to be applied.

	A	B	C	D
1	**Newspaper Sales**	**Jan**	**Feb**	**Mar**
2	The Daily Telegraph	12090	13009	13090
3	The Mail	15102	15602	15765
4	The Guardian	11090	10358	10975
5	Financial Times	8759	9035	8950
6	**Total**	47041	48004	48780

Figure 132

1. Select **T**ools, **O**ptions, choose the | Calculation | tab

2. Click with the left 🖱 button on ☑ Accept labels in formulas

3. Press | OK |

4. Highlight the area A1:D6

5. Select **I**nsert, **N**ame, | Apply... |

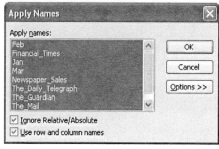

Figure 133

6. Choose | OK |, the names have been applied

7. Select a empty cell, type =The Mail Jan + The Guardian Jan

8. Press Enter

9. The total for The Mail and The Guardian for January are displayed

10. Select cell E2

11. Type =SUM(The Daily Telegraph) or type =The Daily Telegraph Jan + Feb + Mar

12. Press Enter

13. Ensure cell E2 is selected, use the Fill Handle and drag down to cell E5

14. The formulas are applied to the cells using the Applied Names

Delete a Range of Names

1. Select the row to be deleted
2. Choose, **E**dit, **D**elete
3. If a total displays [#REF!] when a row has been deleted
4. The totals will need to be recalculated
5. Select the area A1:E4
6. Click **I**nsert, **N**ame, **C**reate

Figure 134

7. Choose [OK]
8. The following dialog box appears

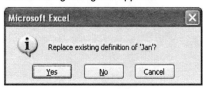

Figure 135

9. Select [Yes] on all occasions
10. Select **I**nsert, **N**ame, **A**pply
11. Choose [OK]
12. Save the workbook as Working with Names and Ranges.xls

Displaying Range Names

To view an index of the range names applied in a worksheet

1. Click in the empty cell H1 to display the information

2. Select Insert,  Name ▶ , Paste...

Paste name
Feb
Financial_Times
Jan
Mar
Newspaper_Sales
The_Daily_Telegraph
The_Guardian
The_Mail

Figure 136

3. Select Paste List

4. The applied names and references are displayed

	H	I
1	Feb	=Sheet1!$C$2:$C$6
2	Financial_Times	=Sheet1!$B$5:$D$5
3	Jan	=Sheet1!$B$2:$B$6
4	Mar	=Sheet1!$D$2:$D$6
5	Newspaper_Sales	=Sheet1!$B$2:$D$6
6	The_Daily_Telegraph	=Sheet1!$B$2:$D$2
7	The_Guardian	=Sheet1!$B$4:$D$4
8	The_Mail	=Sheet1!$B$3:$D$3
9	Total	=Sheet1!$B$6:$D$6

Figure 137

Note: **The list will not automatically update if new names are added.**

Creating **Range Labels**

A Range Label is a way of using information from a row or column heading. Once a label has been created, calculating information from the label can be used as a reference in a formula rather than the cell reference. Range Labels are displayed with a blue border when the zoom area is reduced to below 40%.

Creating a Range Label

1. Open a New Workbook
2. Create the following information

	A	B	C	D	E
1		January	February	March	April
2	Sales Area A	23	75	83	45
3	Sales Area B	134	47	34	56
4	Sales Area C	34	89	117	45

Figure 138

3. Select Insert, Name | Label... |
4. The Label Ranges dialog box appears

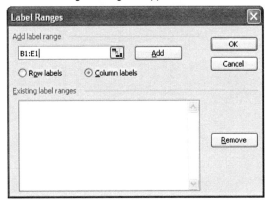

Figure 139

5. Choose the label range by selecting the 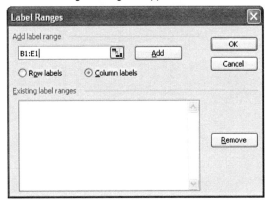 icon
6. Highlight cells B1:E1
7. Click on the to return to the Label Ranges dialog box
8. Choose | ⊙ Column labels |
9. Select | Add |
10. The range appears in the Existing label ranges
11. Re-select the label range by selecting the

12. Highlight A2:A4

13. Click on the ▤ to return to the Label Ranges dialog box

14. Select ⊙ Row labels , press [Add]

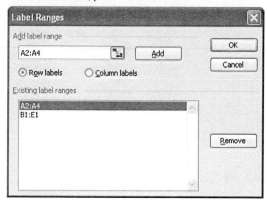

Figure 140

15. Click [OK]

16. Select **V**iew, **Z**oom, **C**ustom

17. Change the percentage to less than 40% ⊙ Custom: 39 %

18. Choose [OK], the label ranges are highlighted in blue

19. Change the percentage back to 100%

20. Select **T**ools, **O**ptions, [Calculation]

21. Tick ☑ Accept la**b**els in formulas, choose [OK]

22. In cell A6 type the heading Totals

23. Select cell B6, type =sum(January)

24. The result of 191 is the sum of B2:B4

25. Re-select cell B6

26. Use the Fill Handle to drag and copy the formula from B6 to E6

27. Click cells C6, D6 and E6, the formula relates to the Column Labels

28. Select cell F2, create the formula =sum(Sales Area A)

29. Create the formula for cells F3 and F4

30. Click in a cell of your choice

31. Type =sum(Sales Area B March)+(Sales Area C April), press Enter

32. Save the workbook Using Range Labels.xls

Working with Duplicate Labels

If a worksheet contains duplicate Range Labels and a formula has been entered using the same named label, Excel displays the Identify Label dialog box for the user to select the cell containing the label to be used.

Identifying Duplicate Labels

1. Open up the workbook Using Range Labels.xls

2. Select cell B9, type April

3. Re-select the cell, create a Range Label

4. Select Insert, Name, | Label... |

5. The Label Ranges dialog box appears

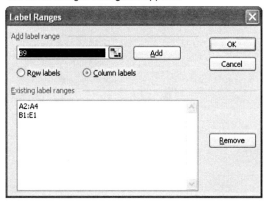

Figure 141

6. Choose ⦿ Column labels

7. Select | Add |, choose | OK |

8. Enter numeric values in cells, B10:B12

9. Select a cell, type =sum(April)

10. The Identify Label dialog box appears

Figure 142

11. Choose E1 as the label range by selecting the 🔲 icon

12. Click on the 🔲 to return to the Label Ranges dialog box

13. Click ⌈ OK ⌋

14. The result of the formula appears using the Label April

Using the Auditing Functions

Excel allows formulas and results in a worksheet to be traced using the Auditing Toolbar.

Figure 143

Using Trace Precedent and Dependent Features

1. Create the following worksheet

	A	B	C	D	E	F	G
1	Sales	Jan	Feb	Mar	Apr	May	Total
2							
3	Monday	11500	14000	11125	11765	15122	63512
4	Tuesday	12000	14001	13234	11000	13245	63480
5	Wednesday	14000	14002	12678	11200	19174	71054
6	Thursday	16000	14003	10976	11300	13328	65607
7	Friday	18000	14004	16740	11400	19884	80028
8	Saturday	20000	14005	10308	11500	19487	75300
9	Sunday	22000	14006	13444	11600	16029	77079
10							
11	Monthly Total	113500	98021	88505	79765	116269	

Figure 144

2. Select cell G3, click on the Trace Precedents 📊 icon

3. Tracer arrows display the cells that provide data to the formula

	A	B	C	D	E	F	G
1	Sales	Jan	Feb	Mar	Apr	May	Total
2							
3	Monday	11500	14000	11125	11765	15122	63512

Figure 145

4. To remove the arrows click on the Remove Precedent Arrows 📊 icon

5. Select cell C6, click on the Trace Dependents ⌨ icon

	A	B	C	D	E	F	G
1	Sales	Jan	Feb	Mar	Apr	May	Total
2							
3	Monday	11500	14000	11125	11765	15122	63512
4	Tuesday	12000	14001	13234	11000	13245	63480
5	Wednesday	14000	14002	12678	11200	19174	71054
6	Thursday	16000	14003	10976	11300	13320	65607
7	Friday	18000	14004	16740	11400	19884	80028
8	Saturday	20000	14005	10308	11500	19487	75300
9	Sunday	22000	14006	13444	11600	16029	77079
10							
11	Monthly Total	113500	98021	88505	79765	116269	

Figure 146

6. Tracer arrows highlight the cells containing data to the formula

7. To remove the arrows click on the Remove Dependent Arrows ⌨ icon

8. Save the Workbook as Using Auditing Functions.xls

Using Trace Error Features

1. If an error occurs, select the cell containing the error message

2. Choose the Error Checking 📵 icon

3. The Error Checking dialog box appears, displaying the cell reference

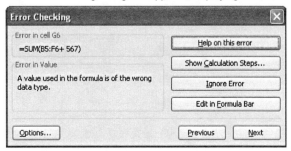

Figure 147

4. Choose [Next] to identify the type of error

5. Press [Edit in Formula Bar]

6. Amend the reference manually

7. Select the ☑ to accept the change, choose [Resume]

8. Click [Next]

Figure 148

9. Click [OK]

Note: **The Trace Error Feature will display errors in any worksheet within an open workbook. If formulas are contained in another workbook that workbook needs to be opened to complete the full check.**

Using the Watch Window

1. Open the Workbook named Using Auditing Functions.xls

2. Select Show Watch Window  icon from the Formula Auditing Toolbar

3. The Watch Window dialog box appears

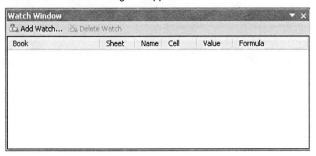

Figure 149

4. Highlight cells G3:G9, choose [Add Watch...]

5. The Add Watch window appears

Figure 150

6. Click [Add]

7. The highlighted cells appear in the Watch Window

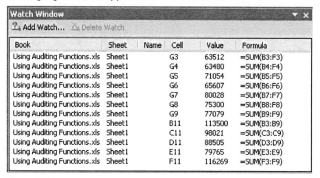

Figure 151

8. Select cell F11, create the formula for Sales in May

9. Repeat the process to add F11 to the Watch Window

10. To delete a Watch Window, select item to delete, choose ☒ Delete Watch

Items within the Watch Window

1. This displays the name of the Workbook, Sheet, Cell, Value and Formula

2. The user can watch cells and their formulas even when out of view

3. To display formulas in another workbook, the workbook must be opened

4. A defined name for a formula is displayed in the ⌊ Name ⌋ area

5. To sort by value, select ⌊ Value ⌋

Strings and Text Functions

A string is a sequence of characters that can be entered as a label in Excel. If a label is used to produce a formula it is referred to as a String Value. Formulas that contain more than one string value are referred to as string expressions and must begin with an = (equal symbol). String expressions are often joined together and referred to as Concatenated. The following example displays how concatenation works.

	A	B	C	D	E
1	First Name	Surname	Result	Formula	Explanation
2	Robert	Smith	Robert Smith	=A2&" "&B2	Joins cells A2 & B2 with a space between cells
3	Peter	Richards	PETER RICHARDS	=UPPER(A3&" "&B3)	Upper case, join cells A3 & B3, space between cells
4	Tony	Parker	tony parker	=LOWER(A4&" "&B4)	Lower case, join cells A4 & B4, space between cells
5	Andrew	Brown	Andrew Brown	=PROPER(A5&" "&B5)	Initial caps join cells A5 & B5, space between cells
6	Bobby	Ainge	12	=LEN(A6&" "&B6)	Number of characters in cells A6 & B6 plus any hidden characters
7	bobby	ainge	Bobby Ainge	=TRIM(PROPER(A7&" "&B7))	No hidden characters, initial caps, display A7 & B7

Figure 152

Functions are organised by category, such as Text and Logical (whether an argument is true or false), an argument can be numbers, text, logical values, tables or functions. A function is made up of **Function_Name(argument1, argument2 .....)**, an argument is the information that a function uses to produce a **New Value** or perform an action.

Using the Function Wizard

The Function Wizard provides an easy guide to creating all formulas.

1. Click in a cell
2. Choose Insert, ⨍ₓ Function...
3. The Insert Function dialog box appears
4. Alternatively click on the Insert Function ⨍ₓ icon on the Formula bar
5. In the Search for a function box type "Text in upper case", press Go
6. The Function Wizard highlights the appropriate function name

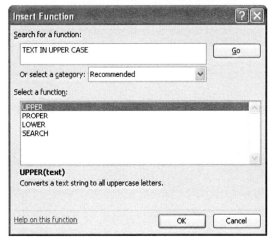

Figure 153

7. Click OK
8. The Function Arguments dialog box appears

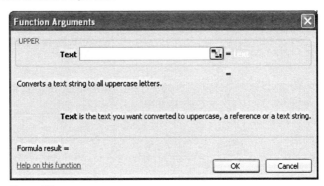

Figure 154

9. In the text box type smart pc guides

10. Click [OK]

11. The text appears in uppercase

12. The formula is =UPPER("smart pc guides")

Exercise 9: - Using the Function Wizard

1. Create the following table in a New Worksheet, using the Function Wizard and Quick Reference Formula

Department	Names		Quick Reference
Human Resources			Create in Uppercase
HR DiRector	ChArlEs kingFisher		Create in Proper
HR CONtroller	ANNe SparRow		Create in Initial Caps
hr officer	john Starling		Create in Lowercase
HR Administrator	JUDY Crow		Initial Caps
HR CLERK	HARry SWift		Create in Uppercase

2. Update the table as follows

3. Replace Director with Manager

4. Replace Administrator with Assistant

5. Replace hr officer with initial caps

6. Using Concatenate, add Robert Bird as an additional Manager

7. Insert a column to display a copy of each working formula

8. The results from the exercise are displayed below

Department	Names
HUMAN RESOURCES	
HR Manager	Charles Kingfisher/Robert Bird
HR Controller	Anne Sparrow
HR Officer	john starling
HR Assistant	Judy Crow
HR CLERK	HARRY SWIFT

9. Save the worksheet Working with the Function Wizard.xls

Search and Find Functions

The search function defined as *Search* is not case sensitive and allows a character or text string to be located, whereas the find function *Find* can be used to locate a character or text string but is case sensitive.

Working with Search and Find

The following table provides a brief example of how the search and find functions work. It is important to plan the formula, brackets are colour coded $\boxed{=(((()))))}$ and where brackets have been opened, the same amount of brackets must be closed.

	A	B	C	D
1	Name	Result	Formula	Explanation
2	SMART GUIDES	6	=SEARCH(" ",A2)	Search & display number of characters to space in cell A2
3	SMART GUIDES	6	=FIND(" ",A3)	Find & display number of characters to space in cell A3
4	SMART GUIDES	12	=LEN(A4)	Display number of characters in cell A4
5	SMART GUIDES	6	=LEN(A5)-SEARCH(" ",A5)	Search and display number of characters after the space
6	SMART GUIDES	6	=LEN(A6)-FIND(" ",A6)	Find and display number of characters after the space
7	SMART GUIDES	GUIDES	=RIGHT(A7,LEN(A7)-SEARCH(" ",A7))	Search and display from the right number of characters after the space
8	SMART GUIDES	GUIDES	=RIGHT(A8,LEN(A8)-FIND(" ",A7))	Find and display from the right characters after the space
9	SMART GUIDES	SMART	=LEFT(A9,SEARCH(" ",A9))	Search and display characters to the left of the space
10	SMART GUIDES	SMART	=LEFT(A10,FIND(" ",A10))	Find and display characters to the left of the space
11	SMART GUIDES	Smart	=PROPER(LEFT(A11,SEARCH(" ",A11)))	Search and display the characters to the left of the space in initial caps
12	SMART GUIDES	Guides	=PROPER(RIGHT(A12,LEN(A12)-FIND(" ",A12))))	Find and display from the right characters after the space in initial caps

Figure 155

Exercise 10: - Working with Search and Find

1. Open a New Workbook
2. Type out your first name and surname in a cell of your choice
3. Showing working formulas, find the number of characters in the cell
4. Find the number of characters from the left of the space
5. Search and display in lowercase the characters to the right of the space
6. Search and display in uppercase the characters to the left of the space
7. Save the workbook as Search and Find.xls

Logical Functions

The "**IF**" function allows users to construct and analyse a formula's validity performing an action that calculates whether a statement is TRUE or FALSE. Up to seven **IF** statements can be grouped together (Nested) to construct a more detailed result. To test a statement, Excel evaluates a logical equation returning the word TRUE if the formula statement is true or FALSE if the statement is false.

Description	Symbol Used
Equal to	=
Greater than	>
Less than	<
Not equal to	<>
Greater than or equal to	>=
Less than or equal to	<=

Figure 156

Using the IF Function

1. Open a New Workbook, create the following information

	A	B	C	D
1		**Examination Results**		
2	Description	Pass Rate	Result	Formula
3	Distinction	75%		
4	Pass	63%		
5	Fail	43%		
6	Resit	12%		
7		**Delegates**		
8	John Smith	30%		
9	Jane Thomas	61%		
10	Paul Waters	86%		

Figure 157

2. Select cell C8

3. Following the formula below, generate the results for the 3 delegates

	A	B	C	D
1				**Examination Results**
2	Description	Pass Rate	Result	Formula
3	Distinction	75%	Distinction	
4	Pass	63%	Pass	
5	Fail	43%	Fail	
6	Resit	12%	Resit	
7				**Delegates**
8	John Smith	30%	Resit	=IF(B8>=75%,"Distinction",IF(B8>=63%,"Pass",IF(B8>=43%,"Fail","Resit")))
9	Jane Thomas	61%	Fail	=IF(B9>=75%,"Distinction",IF(B9>=63%,"Pass",IF(B9>=43%,"Fail","Resit")))
10	Paul Waters	86%	Distinction	=IF(B10>=75%,"Distinction",IF(B10>=63%,"Pass",IF(B10>=43%,"Fail","Resit")))

Figure 158

4. Save the workbook as Working with Nested Statements.xls

Exercise 11: - Creating Nested Statements

1. Open a New Workbook

2. Create a table displaying bank interest rates on a current account

3. Use the following rates

Rates	
2%	<=1000
3%	>2000
4%	>4345
5%	>6420

Note: **When using IF statements work from the HIGHEST VALUE downwards, make sure the percentage values are between inverted commas.**

4. Create IF Statements for the following amounts

Current Account (£)	
2000	
4500	
6690	
63	

5. Save the workbook Working with Nested Statements.xls

Using Outlining in Worksheets

Excel allows the user to create summary reports by using the Outline Function to show or hide data. This is achieved by grouping data by column or rows using Automatic Outline or Manual Outline.

Creating an Automatic Outline

1. Open a New Workbook

2. Create the following information

	A	B	C	D	E	F	G	H	I	J
1		January	February	March	QTR 1 Total	April	May	June	QTR 2 Total	Grand Total
2	Sales Team A	£12,567	£13,987	£14,654	£41,208	£11,346	£12,432	£14,165	£37,943	£120,359
3	Sales Team B	£13,909	£12,976	£11,456	£38,341	£10,954	£11,675	£9,197	£31,826	£108,508
4	Sales Team C	£12,543	£12,788	£11,676	£37,007	£13,543	£10,456	£9,329	£33,328	£107,342
5	Sales Team D	£11,905	£12,765	£11,324	£35,994	£10,469	£11,232	£11,190	£32,891	£104,879
6	Total Sales	£50,924	£52,516	£49,110	£152,550	£46,312	£45,795	£43,881	£135,988	£441,088

Figure 159

3. Click anywhere in the data to be outlined

4. Choose, **D**ata, **G**roup and Outline, **A**uto Outline

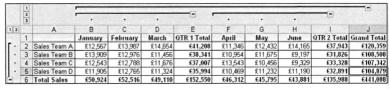

Figure 160

5. The horizontal outlines are displayed above the column

6. The vertical outlines are displayed to the left of the rows

7. In the horizontal area, choose ① to view Grand Totals

8. The ⊞ sign indicates that there is more information that can be displayed

9. Click on the ⊞ to expand hidden information

10. The ⊟ indicates that all information is displayed

11. Click ⊟ to collapse and hide grouped information

12. Press ②, this displays Qtr 1, Qtr 2 and Grand Totals

13. Choose ③ to display all the information

14. Repeat the process for the Vertical Outline area

15. To clear the outline select **D**ata, **G**roup and Outline, **C**lear Outline

16. Save the workbook as Using Outlines.xls

Exercise 12: - Creating a Manual Outline

Manual Outline is a way by which the user controls the information that is to be grouped together. The Manual Outline can also be used in conjunction with the Automatic Outline.

1. Open the workbook Using Outlines.xls
2. Select cells B1:D1
3. Choose, Data, Group and Outline, Group
4. The Group dialog box appears
5. Select Columns

6. Click OK
7. Repeat the process for cell F1:H1
8. The horizontal outlines are displayed above the columns headings
9. Select B1:I1, create a Manual Column Outline
10. Select A2:A5, group the rows to create a Vertical Outline
11. Save the workbook Using Outlines.xls

Consolidation of Data

The Consolidation Feature enables data to be combined from independent workbooks or different worksheets.

1. Open a New Workbook

2. In the worksheet create the following using formulas where applicable

	A	B	C	D	E	F
1	MS Office 2000					
2		Qtr 1	Qtr 2	Qtr 3	Qtr 4	Total
3	Word	100	200	300	400	1000
4	Excel	100	200	300	400	1000
5	PowerPoint	75	75	80	125	355
6	Access	50	40	35	27	152
7	Project	25	40	50	60	175

Figure 161

3. Highlight cells A2:F7

4. Select Insert, Name, Define

5. Type the name as Table

6. Click [Add], press [OK]

7. Create a folder named Consolidation to store the workbooks

8. Save the workbook as MS Office 2000 Courses.xls

9. Close the workbook

10. Repeat the process for MS Office XP and MS Office 2003

	A	B	C	D	E	F
1	MS Office XP					
2		Qtr 1	Qtr 2	Qtr 3	Qtr 4	Total
3	Word	100	200	300	400	1000
4	Excel	100	200	300	400	1000
5	PowerPoint	75	75	80	125	355
6	Access	50	40	35	27	152
7	Project	25	40	50	60	175

Figure 162

	A	B	C	D	E	F
1	MS Office 2003					
2		Qtr 1	Qtr 2	Qtr 3	Qtr 4	Total
3	Word	100	200	300	400	1000
4	Excel	100	200	300	400	1000
5	PowerPoint	75	75	80	125	355
6	Access	50	40	35	27	152
7	Project	25	40	50	60	175

Figure 163

11. Open a New Workbook

12. Click in cell A1

13. Select **D**ata, Co**n**solidate

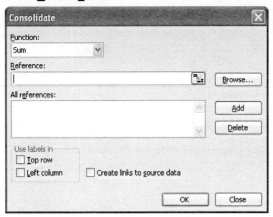

Figure 164

14. In the **F**unction area select SUM

15. Press [Browse...] to locate MS Office 2000 Courses.xls

16. Select the file, choose [OK]

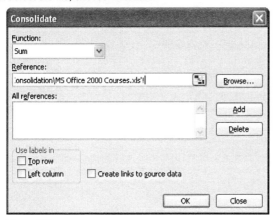

Figure 165

17. Type the word Table after the file name as shown below

Figure 166

18. Click [Add] to save the reference

19. Repeat steps 15 to 18 for MS Office XP and MS Office 2003

20. Select Use Labels, tick **T**op row and **L**eft column

21. Tick Create links to **s**ource data as shown

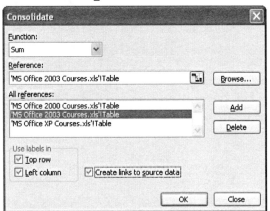

Figure 167

22. Select [OK], the consolidated worksheet appears

1 2		A	C	D	E	F	G
	1		Qtr 1	Qtr 2	Qtr 3	Qtr 4	Total
+	5	Word	300	600	900	1200	3000
+	9	Excel	300	600	900	1200	3000
+	13	PowerPoint	225	225	240	375	1065
+	17	Access	150	120	105	81	456
+	21	Project	75	120	150	180	525

Figure 168

23. Use the outline ⊞ and ⊟ signs to reveal or collapse the linked data

24. Save the workbook Consolidation of Data.xls

25. If a workbooks data is updated at any time when the consolidated worksheet is opened, the following prompt appears

Figure 169

26. Click [Update]

Templates

A template is a means of creating a workbook that is consistent allowing such documents as Invoices, Timesheets and Balance Sheets to be used with preset styles and formatting. When a new workbook is generated as a template it is used as the basis for the worksheet. Templates are saved to the Normal general area; however, it is possible to create a new tab for an organisation in the templates area that allows company templates to be quickly identified.

To save a Workbook as a Template

1. Select File, Save As
2. Save as SMART PC Guides Timesheet
3. Click on the ⌄ in the Save as type: area
4. Select Template to move to the 🗁 Templates area
5. In the Template folder, click on the New Folder 🗂 icon
6. In the Name area type SMART PC Guides Template

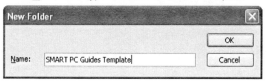

Figure 170

7. Press OK
8. Save and close the template
9. To view the template Select File, New
10. Select 🔲 On my computer... in the template area
11. Choose the tab SMART PC Guides Template

Figure 171

12. Select the SMART PC Guides Timesheet Template
13. Click OK to open a new workbook based on the template

Exercise 13: - Open and Amend an Existing Template

This exercise demonstrates how a template can be customised quickly.

1. Choose File, New

2. Select [On my computer...] from the Templates Task Pane area

3. choose the tab named [Spreadsheet Solutions]

4. Double click on Sales Invoice

5. Press Tools, Protection, Unprotect Sheet

6. Use [F5] key to go to C3

7. Change font to Arial 14, Blue, Bold

8. Type out the name of your organisation

9. Select E15 change State to Country

10. Go to G15 change ZIP to Postcode

11. In cell M13 format the date type as [dd/mm/yyyy]

12. Select cell L19 change the currency to £ symbol

13. Copy the format from L19:L35

14. In M19 type 10.00

15. Using Format Cells change the currency £ symbol

16. Use Format Painter to copy the format of M19:M36 and M38:M40

17. Change M37 to the currency £ symbol

18. Delete the information in J38 type VAT

19. In L38 type 17.5%

20. Delete any figures in L19 and M19

21. Press Tools, Protection, Protect Sheet

22. Choose [OK]

23. Name the template as SMART PC Guides Invoice.xlt

24. Save the template in the SMART PC Guides templates area

25. Close the workbook

26. Re-open the template from the [SMART PC Guides Template] tab

Using Scenario Manager

The Scenario Manager is part of the What If analysis. Each scenario that is added to the Scenario Manager has a defined name applied to the data. By grouping data it is possible to use the Scenario Manager to display the outcome of what will happen to the worksheet if the data from a scenario is applied.

Creating Scenarios in a Workbook

1. Open a New Workbook

2. Create the following information, name the worksheet Project Expenses

	A	B
1	**Company Express**	**Daily Costs**
2	Project Expenses Allowance	£200.00
3	Hotel Accommodation	£100.00
4	Mobile Phone Calls	£15.75
5	Petrol	£35.00
6	Evening Meal Allowance	£28.45
7	Taxis	£14.80
8	**Total**	£194.00
9		
10	Outstanding Allowance	£6.00

Figure 172

3. Choose cell B2, select Insert, Name, Define

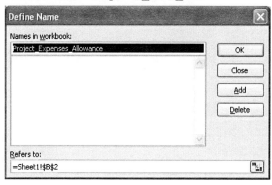

Figure 173

4. Click [Add], [OK]

5. Repeat steps 3 and 4 for cells B3:B8 and B10

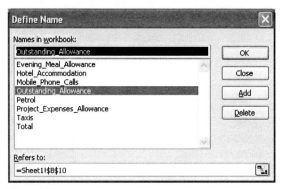

Figure 174

6. Select **T**ools, Sc**e**narios, the Scenario Manager dialog box appears

Figure 175

7. Press [Add...]

8. Type Normal Values in the Scenario **n**ame area

9. Select the 🔲 icon, highlight cells B2:B7

10. Press 🔲 to return to the Edit Scenario dialog box

Figure 176

11. Click 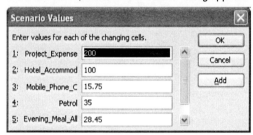, the Scenario Values dialog appears

Figure 177

12. Click , to return to the Scenario Manager dialog box

Figure 178

13. Repeat steps 7 to 12 to generate a Most Expensive Scenario

14. Change the values as below

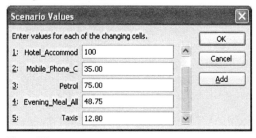

Figure 179

15. Create a Least Expensive Scenario, change the values as below

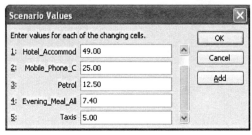

Figure 180

16. Click [OK] to display the Scenario Manager

Display the Scenarios

1. Choose the Most Expensive Scenario, click [Show]

Figure 181

2. The data in the worksheet changes and is displayed

	A	B
1	**Company Express**	**Daily Costs**
2	Project Expenses Allowance	£200.00
3	Hotel Accommodation	£100.00
4	Mobile Phone Calls	£35.00
5	Petrol	£75.00
6	Evening Meal Allowance	£48.75
7	Taxis	£12.80
8	**Total**	£271.55
9		
10	Outstanding Allowance	-£71.55

Figure 182

3. Repeat the process for the other scenarios
4. Re-select the Scenario Normal Values, press [Show]
5. To view a summary of the results, select [Summary...]

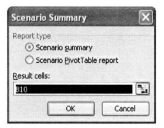

Figure 183

6. Choose Report type Scenario **s**ummary

7. Click [OK]

8. The Scenario Summary is displayed on a separate worksheet

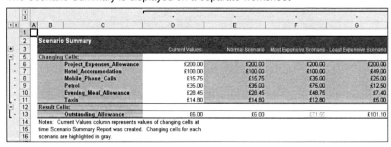

Figure 184

9. Vertical and Horizontal Outlines enable data to be expanded or collapsed

10. Save the Workbook as Creating Scenarios.xls, close the workbook

Custom Views

Custom Views allows the user to store, format and print options by selection and applies a name to a particular view.

Creating a Custom View

1. Open the workbook Creating Scenarios.xls

2. Select the worksheet named Project Expenses

3. Highlight cells A1:B8

4. Select **V**iew, [Custom **V**iews...]

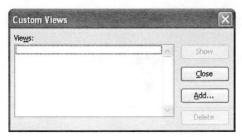

Figure 185

5. Click 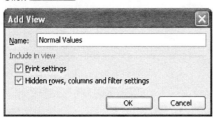 Add...

Figure 186

6. Type the name as Normal Values, click [OK]

7. Choose the worksheet named Scenario Summary, highlight cells B2:G13

8. Select **V**iew, Custom **V**iews, the Custom Views dialog box appears

9. Press [Add...]

10. Name the View as Scenario Summary Sheet, click [OK]

11. Save to update the workbook Creating Scenarios.xls

Displaying a Custom View

1. Select **V**iew, Custom **V**iews, the Custom Views dialog box appears

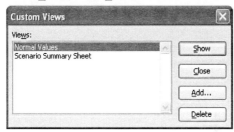

Figure 187

2. Select the view to be displayed

3. Click [Show], the defined area is displayed and highlighted

Pivot Tables

The Pivot Table Function allows data to be viewed from a different perspective. The report appears in a table format whereby the user decides the location of the data within the workbook.   The Pivot Table Function automatically applies formatting to the information used. All Pivot Tables need to be planned to decide what information needs to be displayed.

Creating a Pivot Table

1. Open up a New Workbook, create the following information

	A	B	C	D	E	F
1	Name	Employee Number	Date Hired	Department	Job Title	Current Salary
2	Paul Smith	1	10/01/1965	Marketing	Marketing Administrator	£15,122
3	Jane Barrow	2	11/02/1999	Sales	Sector Director	£43,300
4	Rachael Jones	3	04/03/1990	IT	IT Helpdesk	£23,578
5	Robert Williams	4	03/02/2000	Human Resources	HR Manager	£30,500
6	James Harrow	5	22/04/1996	Marketing	Brand Manager	£27,498
7	Hannah Brown	6	10/07/1997	Marketing	Marketing Assistant	£12,750
8	Ruth Powers	7	21/02/1976	Accounts	Account Handler	£16,029

Figure 188

2. Click in the data area

3. Select **D**ata, [icon] PivotTable and PivotChart Report…

4. Step 1 of the Wizard appears

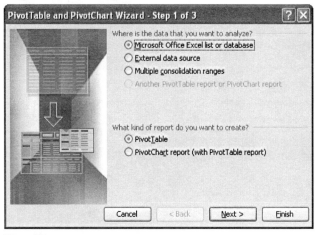

Figure 189

5. Choose Microsoft Excel list or database

6. Select Pivot Table as the type of report to be created

7. Choose [Next >] to go to Step 2

Figure 190

8. The data range is highlighted

9. Press [Next >] to move to Step 3

Figure 191

10. Select ⊙ New worksheet

11. Choose [Layout...] to move to the Layout dialog box

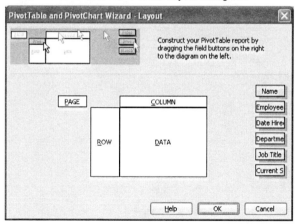

Figure 192

12. Drag the field buttons from the right into the diagram area as shown below

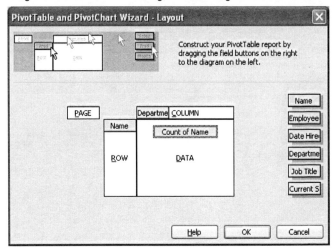

Figure 193

13. Click [OK]

14. Select [Finish]

15. The information is displayed in a separate worksheet

16. In cell B3, click on the downward remove the tick from show all

17. Choose Marketing, click [OK]

18. The Pivot Table displays the staff in Marketing

	A	B
1	Department	Marketing ▼
2		
3	Count of Name	
4	Name ▼	Total
5	Hannah Brown	1
6	James Harrow	1
7	Paul Smith	1
8	Grand Total	3

Figure 194

19. Repeat these steps to display the other departments

20. Information can be quickly restructured to display a different set of data

21. Select [PivotTable ▼] from the Pivot Table toolbar

22. Choose [PivotTable Wizard]

23. Select , change the layout as shown

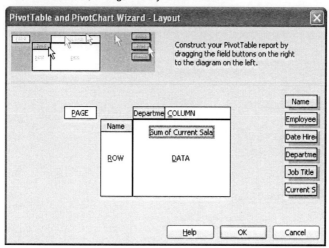

Figure 195

24. Click [OK], [Finish]

	A	B	C	D	E	F	G
3	Sum of Current Salary	Department ▼					
4	Name ▼	Human Resources	Accounts	IT	Marketing	Sales	Grand Total
5	Hannah Brown				12750		12750
6	James Harrow				27498		27498
7	Jane Barrow					43300	43300
8	Paul Smith				15122		15122
9	Rachael Jones			23578			23578
10	Robert Williams	30500					30500
11	Ruth Powers		16029				16029
12	Grand Total	30500	16029	23578	55370	43300	168777

Figure 196

25. Save the workbook as Working with Pivot Tables.xls

Using the Wizard to Change a Pivot Table

1. Click anywhere in the Pivot Table, the Pivot Table Toolbar appears

Figure 197

2. Select Pivot Table, choose [PivotTable Wizard] to go to Step 3

3. [Layout...] enables the user to amend the structure of the Pivot Table

4. [< Back] or [Next >] enables the steps of the wizard to be traced

Customising Pivot Table Detail

1. Open Working with Pivot Tables.xls

2. Click in the Pivot Table, select [⚙ Field Settings...] from the Pivot Table toolbar

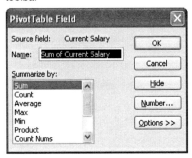

Figure 198

3. Press [Number...], choose Currency

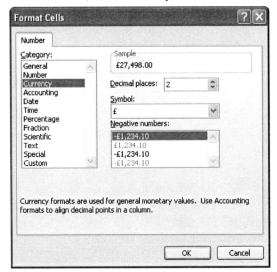

Figure 199

4. Click [OK] twice

5. The Currency format is applied to the Pivot Table

6. Save the workbook

7. Click anywhere in the Pivot Table, select the Format Report 🔲 icon

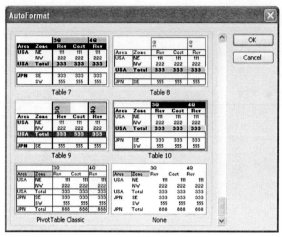

Figure 200

8. Choose the required format

9. Click [OK], the select format is applied

10. Go back to the original data

11. Change Hannah Brown's Salary to £19500

12. Click in the Pivot Table

13. Select the Refresh Data 🔔 icon

14. The Pivot Table is updated to display the amended salary

15. Save the Workbook

Creating a Chart from Pivot Table

1. Click in the Pivot Table

2. Select the 📊 icon from the Pivot Table toolbar

3. The chart is displayed on a separate worksheet

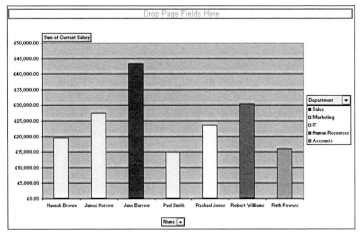

Figure 201

4. Select the downward arrow in the Chart for Department

5. Click with the left button to deselect the items not required in the chart

Figure 202

6. Click OK

7. Switch back to the worksheet containing the Pivot Table

8. The Pivot Table displays a mirror image of the charted information

Sum of Current Salary	Department			
Name	Human Resources	IT	Marketing	Grand Total
Hannah Brown			12500	12500
James Harrow			27498	27498
Paul Smith			15122	15122
Rachael Jones		23578		23578
Robert Williams	30500			30500
Grand Total	30500	23578	55120	109198

Figure 203

9. Select Department and Show All

10. Click [OK], all the information is available

Macros

A Macro is a way whereby commands, keystrokes, and actions can be recorded to automate specific tasks.

Preparation Work before Recording a Macro

1. Write down each step of the macro
2. What should the macro do?
3. Where should the macro be stored?
4. Does the macro need to be available to other workbooks?
5. Does formatting need to be applied?
6. Does the macro need to be applied to specific cells (absolute)?
7. Does the macro need to be applied to any cells (relative)?
8. Provide an appropriate name to identify the macro
9. Do a walkthrough of the steps before recording the macro

Creating a Relative Reference Macro to Format Cells

1. Select **T**ools, **M**acro, [● Record New Macro...]
2. The Record Macro dialog box appears

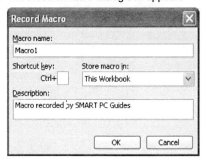

Figure 204

3. Name the macro as Formatting_Cells

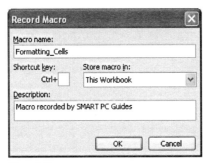

Figure 205

4. Store the macro in This Workbook

5. The description area provides the date the macro was created,

6. Choose [OK]

7. [Recording] appears in the Status Bar area

8. To apply relative referencing click on the ⊞ icon on the Stop Recording Toolbar so that the icon remains with an orange background

9. Select cell A1, choose F**o**rmat, C**e**lls

10. Select the Font tab, change the **C**olour to Blue

11. Select the Number tab, set the options as shown

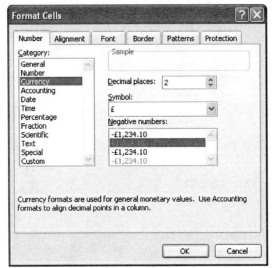

Figure 206

12. Click [OK]

13. Press the Stop Recording ▣ icon

14. In cell A1, type 45, press Return or [Enter]

15. 45 has changed to £45.00 in blue font

16. Delete the information in A1, type -6, press Return, [£6.00] appears in red

17. In a series of cells type the following numbers

Sales A	1	2	3	4	5
Sales B	6	7	8	9	10
Total	7	9	11	13	15

Figure 207

18. Select the cells containing the numbers

19. Select Tools, Macro, Macros

20. Alternatively press [Alt] [F8]

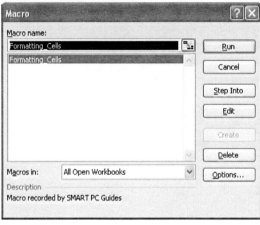

Figure 208

21. Choose the macro named Formatting_Cells

22. Select [Run]

23. The numbers are formatted automatically using the macro

Exercise 14: - Creating a Header & Footer Macro

1. Create a macro and name it Header_Footer
2. Store the macro in Personal Macro Workbook

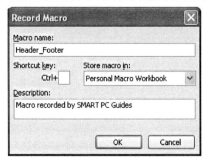

3. Type and centre a heading named SMART PC Guides
4. In the Footer Area type **V1.0**
5. Click Stop Recording
6. Click on a new workbook
7. In cell A1 type =Today() to insert the date
8. Run the macro named Header_Footer
9. Preview the results

Create a Relative Macro for a Web Address

To create a macro to produce a company Web address, the column has to be widened to fully display the address in the cell and the macro stored in the Personal.xls Macro Workbook. When the Macro is stored in the Personal.xls macro workbook, it can be run with every workbook.

1. Select Tools, [Macro ▶], [◉ Record New Macro...]

2. The Record Macro dialog box appears

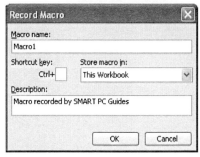

Figure 209

3. Name the macro as Web_Address

4. Store the macro in the Personal Macro Workbook, press [OK]

5. When the macro is recording, [Recording] appears in the Status Bar area

6. To apply relative referencing click on the 🔲 icon on the Stop Recording Toolbar so that the icon remains with an orange background

7. Select cell A1, choose, Insert, Hyperlink

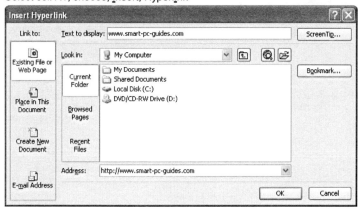

Figure 210

8. Complete the Text to display and Address boxes, press [OK]

9. Widen the column to fit the web address in the cell

10. Press the Stop Recording [■] icon

11. Click on a New Workbook, select [Alt] [F8] or Tools, Macro, Macros

12. Select All Open Workbooks

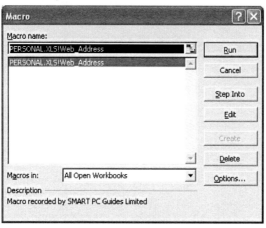

Figure 211

13. Select Personal.xls!Web_Address, press [Run]

14. Select File, Print Preview to view the results of the macro

Deleting a Macro

1. Select [Alt] [F8] or Tools, Macro, Macros

2. Choose the macro to be deleted, select [Delete]

3. The following prompt style dialog appears

Figure 212

4. Choose [Yes], the macro is deleted

Create a Macro to Display Print Area Icon

1. Select **T**ools, [Macro   ▶], [◉   Record New Macro...]

2. The Record Macro dialog box appears

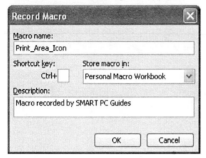

Figure 213

3. Set the **M**acro name as Print_Area_Icon

4. Store the macro in the Personal Macro Workbook, click [OK   ]

5. Choose **V**iew, **T**oolbars, **C**ustomise, select the **C**ommands tab

6. Choose File from the area Cate**g**ories

Figure 214

7. In the Comman**d**s area scroll to the Set Print Area Command

8. Drag to the area displayed in the Formatting Toolbar [**B**   *I*   **U**   图]

9. Click, [Close]

10. Click on the Stop Recording [⬛] icon

11. Open up a New Workbook, highlight the area to print

12. Choose the Set Print area [📖] icon

13. Select **V**iew, **T**oolbars, **C**ustomise

Figure 215

14. Click with the left ⚲ button, drag the Set Print Area off the Formatting Toolbar over the Commands area of the Customise dialog

15. Release the left ⚲ button, the icon is removed from the toolbar

16. Select [Close]

17. Press [Alt] [F8] select the macro named Print_Area_Icon,

18. Click [Run] with the left ⚲ button

19. The Set Print Area [📖] icon is displayed on the Formatting Toolbar

20. Select [Alt] [F8], reselect the Print Area icon

21. Click on the [Options...] icon to set a Shortcut **k**ey

22. Hold down [Shift] on the keyboard, press the letter [P]

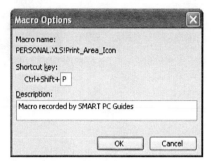

Figure 216

23. Click ⬚ OK ⬚, press ⬚ Cancel ⬚

24. Repeat steps 13 to 16

25. Re-run the macro using the shortcut ⬚ Ctrl ⬚ ⬚ Shift ⬚ ⬚ P ⬚

26. The Set Print Area 🖳 icon re-appears on the Formatting Toolbar

Exercise 15: - Create a Macro to Remove Set Print Icon

1. Press `Ctrl` `Shift` `P` if the 🖼 is not displayed on the Formatting Toolbar

2. Create a macro in the Personal Macro Workbook

3. Name the macro Remove_Print_Area_Icon

4. Select **V**iew, **T**oolbars, **C**ustomise

5. Drag the Set Print Area 🖼 icon off the Formatting Toolbar

6. Click `Close` to remove the Customise dialog and return to the worksheet

7. Click on the Stop Recording ▪ icon

8. Go to the Macro Options area and apply a Shortcut **k**ey as `Shift` `R`

9. The keys to use once the macro has been recorded are displayed

10. Press `Ctrl` `Shift` `P` to display the 🖼 icon

11. `Ctrl` `Shift` `R` will remove the 🖼 icon

What is XML?

XML stands for Extensive Markup Language and is a method use for putting structured data that can found in an Excel worksheet into a text file that follows standard guidelines that can be read by a variety of applications. Users can create customised tags enabling the definition, transmission, validation, and interpretation of data between applications and organisations.

Workbooks or data that was previously difficult to work with can be easily organised by using XML enabling the user to identify and extract specific pieces of data from ordinary documents. For example, reports that contain financial results are no longer static reports as the information they contain can be passed to a database or reused elsewhere, outside of the workbook.

Microsoft Office Excel 2003 XML feature is designed to:

1. Open XML data files into a new workbook

2. Make it easier to import and export data into and out of templates without having to redesign them by mapping XML elements onto existing fields

3. Use XML data as input for your existing calculation models by mapping XML elements onto existing spreadsheet calculation models

4. Map custom XML schemas to data already in your workbooks

5. Incorporate XML data returned form a Web service into your Excel worksheet

How to Use the XML Spreadsheet schema

You can create a workbook in Excel as you normally would and then save it as in the XML Spreadsheet format. Excel uses its own XML schema, XMLSS, to apply XML tags that store information, such as file properties, and define the structure of the workbook.

To Save a Workbook in the XML Spreadsheet Format

1. Select **F**ile, Save **A**s, type the name of the file in the File name box

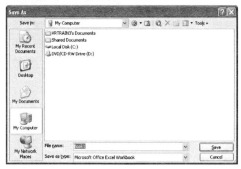

Figure 217

2. Select the location where the information is to be saved

3. In the Save as type box, select XML Spreadsheet

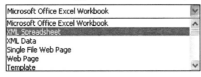

Figure 218

4. Press [Save]

5. The following icon appears in the chosen location

For more information on XML, click the left button on the help icon.

This concludes the Excel 2003 Foundation to Expert Guide. Thank you for choosing Smart PC Guides. For a comprehensive view of Smart PC Guides please visit our website www.smart-pc-guides.com

Notes Pages